# CIRCULAR BREATHING FOR THE FLUTIST

# ROBERT DICK

MULTIPLE BREATH MUSIC COMPANY

Credits:

cover/title page: Sharon Gold

design/paste-up: Lois V Vierk

music copyist: Randa Kirshbaum

photography: Peter Serling

typesetting: Kathy Duncan

© 1987 by Robert Dick

Library of Congress Catalog Card Number: 87-60128
ISBN 0-939407-01-9

All rights reserved. No part of this book may be reproduced or transmitted in any form or by any means, electronic or mechanical, including photocopying, recording, or by any information storage and retrieval system, without permission in writing from the publisher.

## TABLE OF CONTENTS

**INTRODUCTION** ................................................... 5

Chapter I:   Preliminary Observations and
             Basics of the Technique ...................... 9

Chapter II:  Intermediate Phases ........................ 26

Chapter III: Circular Breathing in Orchestral,
             Recital and Concerto Repertoire ......... 35

Chapter IV:  Advanced Technique —
             Circular Breathing in Articulations
             and Extended Techniques ................. 46

**AFTERWORD** ..................................................... 51

# INTRODUCTION

Circular breathing makes it possible to play the flute (or other wind instrument) continuously while inhaling. This seeming contradiction—exhaling to play while inhaling to breathe—is accomplished by storing air in the mouth and cheeks and using this air to play while inhaling through the nose. While this is considered a radically new development in Western classical music, circular breathing is an age-old technique and is the standard method of breathing for the flute in several parts of the world, including the Bulgarian *kaval* and the *narh* flutes of the Indian province of Rajasthan. Glass blowers use circular breathing to maintain continuous air pressure inside molten glass as it is being formed. Circular breathing is found in many ethnic musics, in jazz, the avant-garde and, quite often, in the orchestra. Tubaists have long used circular breathing without fanfare, as have the occasional single and double reed player. Why is the player of the Boehm flute so rarely able to circular breathe? The answers to this question lie in the realms of acoustics and pedagogy. Of all the wind instruments, including the lower brass, the flute uses the most air under the lowest pressure. Since circular breathing is made easier by playing an instrument that uses little air and provides back-pressure, (the oboe being ideal in this way), the flute is problematic. Further, the flute has no mouthpiece to support the lips and no reed to hold to help keep the embouchure shaped correctly while the cheeks are in motion. In trying to learn circular breathing, many have overestimated the importance of the coordinations involved, and focused practice on the coordinations instead of the embouchure development needed. This should be done first, and *then* the coordinations should be applied.

While all the above may seem daunting, circular breathing by no means is an exotic technique limited to the exceptional few. This book presents in detail the learning and practice methods that should enable every flutist to master circular breathing and to apply it in any repertoire. In researching the flute traditions that use circular breathing, I listened to a recording of players from Rajasthan. On first hearing of one of the pieces, I marvelled at the precision, including perfectly matched vibrati, of what I thought was a duo. Upon looking at the photos in the record jacket, I found that the "duo" was one flutist playing two end-blown flutes and circular breathing beautifully on both at once! Suddenly, the Boehm flute just didn't seem that hard any more. The flutist wasn't a professional either, but a shepherd.

For the player of the Boehm flute, circular breathing has musical applications in several spheres. Firstly, it makes possible performance of pieces designed to have phrase lengths longer than the normal breath length. As a composer, I find this freedom invaluable; as a performer, it is indispensable. In traditional classical repertoire, circular breathing can be used in many musically valid ways. The orchestral repertoire is full of famous solos that have very long phrases, phrases that were originally meant to have been played in smaller orchestras, smaller concert halls and on flutes with smaller embouchure holes and correspondingly smaller sounds. With circular breathing, these phrases can be played with a full dynamic range and with freedom from the physical and emotional sense of peril that often occurs. In our solo literature, many similar situations arise. One has only to look at the Bach *Sonatas* for a wide selection of phrases that are just a few beats longer than can be freely accommodated with a normal breath. While the flute and violin were considered interchangeable in the Baroque period, many composers, particularly J.S. Bach, seemed to treat the flute as if it were a wind-powered violin, capable of virtually uninterrupted sound. In these musical situations, the flutist traditionally has had to look for a secondary spot in which to breathe, *and sometimes this secondary spot just doesn't feel right musically*—or, the flutist must face the reality of cutting down on the dynamics at some point in the phrase, going into "air saving mode" in order to get to the musically right place for the breath. Circular breathing will make it possible to place the regular breath in the musically optimal place without having to sacrifice dynamics or expression. The *traverso* does, of course, use less air than its modern counterpart, and much of the problem the current-day flutist encounters in the length of Baroque phrases is due to the change of instrument as well as purely musical issues.

The Boehm flute as interpreted by modern flutemakers features a marvelous array of sound colors and dynamics, but, compared to its nineteenth century forerunners, requires a good deal more air. Playing some of the late nineteenth century *bravura* repertoire on a flute of that period is a revelation; the phrases and air use match perfectly! Playing the same repertoire on a recent flute allows more power, but suddenly some phrases that were comfortable on the older instrument now seem too long. Once again, circular breathing is the technique that provides the freedom for musical answers to musical problems of this type.

In all aspects of our lives as human beings and as flutists, we find ourselves in an environment where the pace of change is accelerating. It is sensible to look ahead and to do our best to prepare for the future. The flute sound of the future will be yet more powerful and colorful, and more capable of projection with presence. Flutists will find themselves needing to answer technical demands of increasing orders of magnitude. Opportunities for futists to perform as recitalists and concerto soloists will continue to expand, with the concurrent need to project to listeners who have become increasingly acclimated to the presence of recordings, and expect the live sound to match the expectations set up by recordings made with close microphone placements. In addressing these challenges, flutists who can circular breathe will find themselves with a distinct technical advantage over those who cannot.

I learned circular breathing from Aurèle Nicolet. In 1978, I had the honor of lecturing to his class in Freiburg, Germany. Afterwards, I asked about circular breathing. Nicolet uses this technique for the endless streams of sixteenth notes in the Bach *Cantatas* and in other classical repertoire. After a brief explanation of the mechanics, he asked me if I felt I understood the process. My reply being affirmative, he smiled and said "Good. It's yours for the doing, *if you do it*". My contribution has been to develop the step-by-step learning process. Circular breathing can now be yours for the doing. It's well worth the effort.

Before moving on into the technique itself, I'd like to add a word about the style of writing I've chosen for this work. Usually, I have an intense dislike of repetition and seek to avoid it. In this book, however, I shall be functioning as teacher and coach, and therefore include the reminders that were found useful both in learning and teaching circular breathing. I have tried to be helpful without being overbearing, and, should you find the occasional line redundant, I am counting on your good graces.

# CHAPTER I

# PRELIMINARY OBSERVATIONS AND BASICS OF THE TECHNIQUE

Learning circular breathing is approached on two levels. The first is to develop the embouchure so that a high quality of tone can be produced while the cheeks and corners of the mouth are moving; the second aspect is to learn the coordinations involved. The learning process of circular breathing is unlike that encountered in acquiring other techniques: it really is not hard to do, yet takes time. This is not paradoxical, it's just that a good deal of the embouchure work takes place as the lip muscles themselves are developed, and this cannot be rushed. Learning involves a commitment of approximately two years in which circular breathing must be practiced daily for ten to fifteen minutes. The two-year span is from day one until circular breathing can be used artistically, beautifully and freely. Circular breathing will gradually become usable in performance long before the two years have passed. I first used circular breathing in public in a limited way, but did so about four months after I began to practice it. The practicing of circular breathing must continue whether or not it is felt that clear progress is being made. There are plateaus in the learning process, and these occur when the focus of development, once again, is in the lip musculature. Further, the embouchure development that begins when practice is started will disappear if you decide to stop working on circular breathing "for a while". Keeping up the practice is the only route to accomplishment. Thus, before starting, several key decisions must be made. Bearing in mind that a two-year effort is not out of proportion to the musical benefits that circular breathing yields for the rest of one's flute playing career, it is vital to decide:

1. To practice circular breathing daily for ten to fifteen minutes, and to give this practice priority, so that it is not missed.

2. Not to be discouraged when—especially in the early going—it may sound (while working on circular breathing) almost as if you have never played before. All of us, quite naturally, have strong emotional links to our sound, and it is difficult to surrender this identity even if only for a short time daily. Have the strength and good humor to recall the joys of being a beginner, especially the excitement of discovery. As soon as daily practice of circular breathing is done, "identity" can instantly be restored.

3. To keep working on circular breathing even if no apparent progress is being made. Only those who give up fail to cross the plateaus in learning this technique. It can be hard to continue without the gratification of clear progress, but remember that when progress is not apparent, the lips are developing as long as the work is kept up.

With these decisions made, preparations for starting are complete. Along the way, as the technique develops, other effects of this practice will begin to appear. Marked improvement in tone quality and in the efficiency of regular breathing are the first signs that the phsyical changes in the embouchure and breathing musculatures are taking place.

## BASIC MECHANICS OF CIRCULAR BREATHING

To circular breathe, the flutist inflates his/her cheeks in a controlled, gradual fashion while playing. Then, the back of the tongue is raised to touch the roof of the mouth at or near the back of the hard palate. The mouth and cheeks now contain a reservoir of air. At the instant that this reservoir is isolated by the tongue's blocking off the back of the mouth, two actions are performed simultaneously: the cheek muscles are used to squeeze the air out of the mouth, continuing the flute sound while a small amount of air is inhaled through the nose. As soon as that air is inhaled, the tongue is lowered, re-opening the normal pathway for exhaling, and the normal breath is "restarted". This cycle is repeated for as long as necessary.

While the basic mechanics of this process are fairly simple, the development of refinements in the technique—the embouchure and breath control needed to seamlessly elide from each part of the cycle into the next—is where time will be spent. In my experience as both student and teacher of circular breathing, I have found that the usual perception—that the coordination should be learned first and the embouchure developed through practicing the coordination—is inaccurate. For the flutist, working without the resistance of a reed or the embouchure support of a mouthpiece, the first issue is to build the embouchure, then apply the coordinations. Following are the exercises that cover the first stages:

Exercise 1: **Playing with the cheeks as full of air as possible**

Play a note, using a pitch between the flute's third octave G♮ and B♮, and see how much air you can let into your cheeks while playing that note. A high pitch is used for two reasons: circular breathing is easier when there is resistance from the instrument, and the top of the flute's third octave is more resistant than lower in the range (the even more resistant fourth octave is too difficult for this purpose). Also, these third octave notes can be produced *forte* with almost no embouchure, just a strong airstream with minimum lip pressure. Play at a full, strong volume so that the air is doing virtually all the work. The lips should be compressed only enough so that they don't flap. The corners of the mouth should be relaxed, much more relaxed than usual. Allow the corners to be moved forward by the inflation of the cheeks and hold the corners together just enough so that they don't leak air. Without the normal embouchure, the tone is not going to sound with its usual quality, and this should not cause concern. Air should be admitted between the upper lip and teeth, and if you find that your upper lip is pushed forward so that it blocks the embouchure hole simply turn the flute outwards until the tone starts. Don't try to make any corrections with the lips at this point. This embouchure is called the **balloon embouchure,** and should be practiced until all of the third octave can be played with the cheeks at maximum inflation. No inhalation through the nose is involved yet, and this won't come into play until the fifth exercise.

This first exercise has an additional meaning along with its function of getting the learning process started, and this is to present the philosophy behind the structure of this learning process. Rather than try to slowly move out from the regularly used embouchure, I find it better to go to the extremes of the embouchure positions first, then to develop refinements and control. In particular "letting go" at the corners of the mouth is a vital step, and a mirror should be used to insure that the corners are relaxed and the cheeks are inflated all the way. When practicing each step of this method, do not ask yourself "Is this amount too much?" but instead, ask "Can I do more?". It is a given that the tone will be radically effected while these exercises are practiced, and this should not be a cause for worry. Think of gradually working back towards the usually produced tone rather than outwards from it.

*High note with regular embouchure*

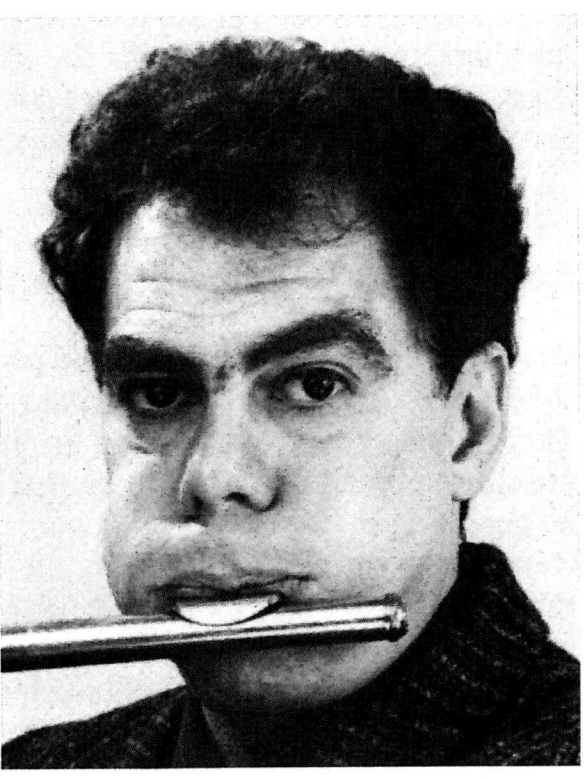
*Same note with inflated cheeks*

Exercise 2: **Bringing the center of the upper lip back to its usual position while keeping the cheeks inflated**

Playing the same third octave note that was used to begin work in the first exercise, release the embouchure at the corners, but now restore the center of the upper lip to its normal position of pressing against the front teeth. In the first exercise, a large gap between the upper lip and teeth should occur as the upper lip inflates along with the cheeks. To close this gap, use the muscles at the center of the upper lip to press that lip against the teeth. Make sure that the upper lip is extended so that the lip opening is not directly at the tips of the teeth, but so that the inner lip surface is extended beyond the tips of the teeth. (This is extremely important for all phases of flute playing, as the amount of inner lip surface available to be shaped into the "lip tube" is proportional to the quality, control and flexibility of the tone.) This pressing action is better described as being done with the musculature located under the nose, the "mustache area", rather than by the lip itself. Remember, it is critical to allow the cheeks to puff out as much as possible because, eventually, the more you can inflate your cheeks, the more time you will have to inhale through the nose.

In practicing this exercise, the center muscles of the embouchure will be working harder than they would in normal playing, in which compression at the corners of the mouth would aid in forming and supporting the embouchure. This is the first stage of the concept and practice of the "work area" of the embouchure moving from the corners (as in normal playing and as in circular breathing when the cheeks are in their deflated position) to the center (when the cheeks are inflated). Again, the idea here is to go to the poles of the motions, then to refine. Practice this exercise until every pitch in the third octave can be played *forte*. This should sound considerably better than exercise 1.

Exercise 3: **Inflating and deflating the cheeks while playing**

Once again, select a high note and play *forte*, but this time, while sustaining the tone, slowly change from the regular embouchure to that outlined in exercise 2. Then while continuing to play, gradually deflate the cheeks, returning to the regular embouchure. The key to this exercise is to make the changes as slowly as possible. At first, the cheeks may tend to move quickly from one position to the other. If the cheeks fill suddenly, the pitch will go flat. This happens because much of the air being exhaled is "diverted" to fill the cheeks, and thus the speed of the airstream at the embouchure is lowered, with a corresponding drop in pitch. The solution is to gradually increase the air pressure while inflating the cheeks (as if making a *crescendo*) just enough to keep the sound at pitch, but not enough to make it louder. Conversely, the pitch will tend to sharpen when the air is squeezed out of the cheeks. Decrease the air pressure just enough to

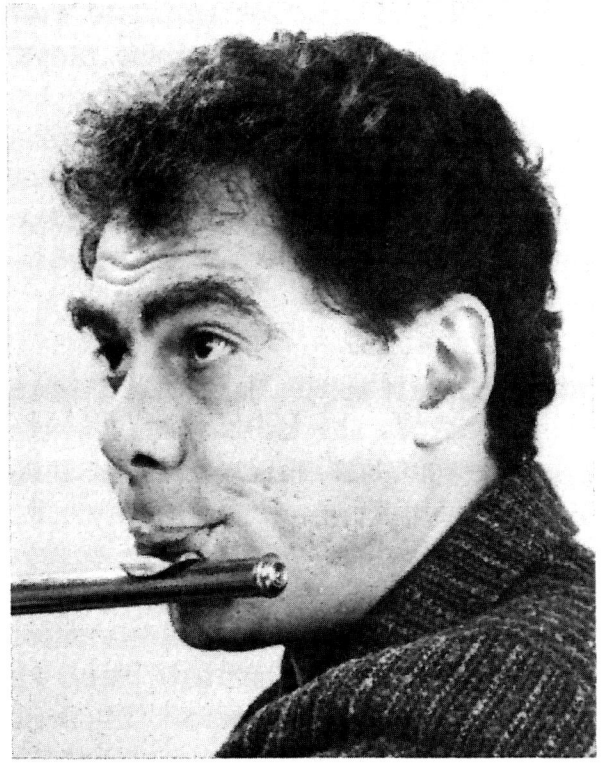 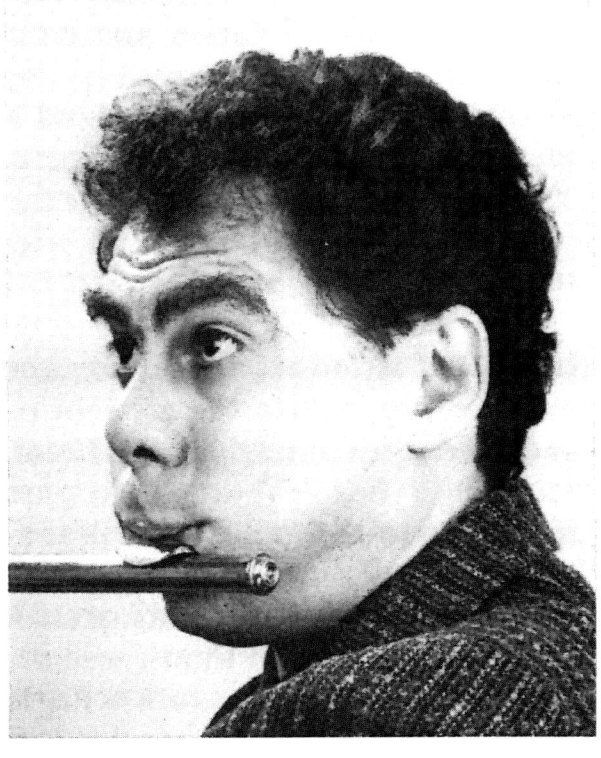

*High note with regular embouchure: note the compression visible at the sides of the embouchure—the center is relatively relaxed*

*The same note with cheeks inflated. Note the compression visible at the center of the embouchure; the corners are relaxed to allow the cheeks to inflate as much as possible.*

keep intonation steady. The cheek muscles play an important part in both the inflation and deflation phases. Neither action is passive, and as the cheek muscles develop, slowing these actions down will become easier. Work on lengthening the time of inflation and deflation to five seconds or longer for each action. This will insure that there will not be sudden "glitches", rapid changes in the embouchure causing the tone to obviously change in loudness, pitch or quality. Practicing very slowly, i.e., taking five or more seconds each to inflate and deflate the cheeks, develops the control needed to perform these actions smoothly at a faster rate later on. When deflating the cheeks, concentrate on keeping the lower lip in contact with the lip plate, as this contact helps maintain the embouchure. When the cheeks are fully inflated and deflation is to begin, start squeezing the cheeks as far back from the embouchure as possible, gradually compressing the cheeks so as to keep the air pressure steady in the forward part of the mouth chamber. The musculature near the embouchure should move at the end of the deflation phase, not the beginning. In inflating the cheeks, the opposite sequence is made. First the musculature near the embouchure moves as the cheeks begin to fill, then the cheeks open up fully from front to back.

Amongst those who do circular breathe on a variety of wind instruments, many "styles" of cheek inflation and deflation can be seen. Some of these players maintain that the air should be stored low in the mouth and cheeks, others maintain the air should be placed high in the cheeks. In each case, the argument is being made for the particular facial structure of the person involved. There is no set "correct" place for the air that applies to everyone. We each have our own facial structure, and, within that structure, wherever the greatest expansion can be made is the correct place for the air.

In the discussion of exercise two, reference was made to the "work area" of the embouchure, and to the concept of its moving from the sides to the center, back and forth during circular breathing. In this exercise, this process is developed and refined. Whatever the particulars of the individual embouchure, it is fair to say that, when playing in the usual manner, not all parts of the embouchure musculature are performing in exactly the same way under exactly the same compression. It is more usual for the muscles at the sides of the mouth to be more compressed than those at the center of the embouchure. Thus, the larger work, the harder task is distributed to the stronger muscles. This is not to say that there is no muscular compression outside the main "work area" of the embouchure. To the contrary, all of the embouchure musculature is involved, whether in compression or rotational action (to turn the lips outwards), but this involvement differs in degree of actual muscle pressure, and the term "work area" (to be used without quotation marks hereafter) is a convenient way to describe the area of primary muscular compression. The embouchure is a marvel of complexity, and very many different muscular actions, some incredibly subtle, act together to produce the embouchure's part in the creation of the sound.

To apply all this to circular breathing, let us describe the sequence of actions in the lip muscles when the cheeks are inflated, then deflated. Beginning with a strong, full sound on the flute's high B♭, for example, the sides of the lips are compressed more than the center, which, to a degree is supported by the airstream. Since this note, when played loudly, is produced more by airspeed than by compression at the center (not so when played softly), a freer sound is made in normal playing when the center is relaxed. However, when inflation is to begin the first step is to slightly firm the muscles at the center of the embouchure. This is done by pressing the center of the upper lip against the teeth above, not at, the aperture, and by compressing the lips together right at the sides of the lip opening (not at the sides of the mouth). Then, allow the muscles on the sides to relax a little bit; this will permit the cheeks to begin to fill towards the front of the mouth. Follow with an increase in compression at the center of the embouchure and a corresponding release at the sides; the cheeks will fill further. This gradual migration of the work area from the corners of the mouth to the center continues until the cheeks are fully inflated. The reason for this migrating action is that a defined embouchure is necessary to produce a high quality sound. Regardless of pitch and/or dynamic level, and no matter how relaxed the embouchure may be in certain cases, a certain degree of muscular definition is always necessary. Thus, as the sides are relaxed to permit the cheeks to inflate, the center of the embouchure must gradually assume the role of defining the lip opening.

At the moment the cheeks are completely full the reverse sequence begins—with each step in squeezing air out of the mouth, a corresponding slight relaxation of the center and a slight firming of the sides is made. All this is done, of course, in concert with the changes in breath pressure, a slight increase while the cheeks are being filled and a slight decrease when the cheeks are being deflated.

After working at *forte* in the upper part of the third octave, begin to practice gradually lower pitches. Also, returning to the upper portion of the third octave, begin to work at lower dynamic levels, taking this a bit at a time. The end-goal of this exercise is to perform good sounding pitches throughout the third octave while making large-scale inflations and deflations of the cheeks. The inflation/deflation process should be ten to fifteen seconds long, and no change in pitch should occur.

Some interesting discoveries in tone quality may be made during the practice of this exercise. When playing high notes *forte*, a clear enrichment in the tone is likely to be heard as the cheeks are inflated. To explain this, a venture into acoustics is in order. When the flute is being played, the mouth functions as one of the important resonators that have great influence on the quality and pitch of the tone. (The other main resonators are the chest cavity and throat, including the vocal chords.[1]) A basic principle of resonators is: when the sound is in the same range as the resonant frequencies of a resonator, then the resonator amplifies the sound, adding energy. It is then sensible to make the mouth resonator larger when playing in its range. Conversely, a resonator will interfere with the sound if it is made too large and the sound is not in the range of its resonant frequencies. In plain English, this means that the sound is improved by inflating the cheeks somewhat in the third octave, with more inflation at the top of that octave than the bottom. The sound will lose some quality if the cheeks are inflated more than a small amount in the flute's first and, to a lesser degree, second octave. When playing, observations should be made about the relationships between pitch and cheek inflation and between dynamics and cheek inflation. The higher and louder the note, up to the top C or C♯, the greater the positive influence cheek inflation will have on the tone.

---

1. For an explication of the influence of the throat and vocal chords on the tone, please see my book **Tone Development Through Extended Techniques,** Multiple Breath Music Co., New York, 1986.

Exercise 4: **Playing the flute using only the air stored in the mouth and cheeks:**

This skill often presents the first real difficulty in learning circular breathing. It may take weeks of ten to fifteen minutes of daily practice. Don't despair if progress is slow; success will come.

To begin, work without the flute. Close the lips and inflate the cheeks. Put the back of the tongue against the roof of the mouth, the same position it would be in to say the word "gong" without releasing the final "ng" sound. The air stored in the cheeks is now isolated, and the sensation is one of having a bag of air in the mouth. To test if the tongue position is correct, inhale through the nose while holding the air in the mouth. If your cheeks do not deflate, the tongue position is correct. If confusion arises, try using a mouthful of water. Hold the water in your mouth and inhale through the nose. (No one ever does this incorrectly more than once.)

Next, try the exercise with the flute. Close the lips, inflate the cheeks, put the tongue in the "gong" position (remembering not to release the final "ng" sound, so that the position is more like "gonnnnn"), and, on any first or second octave note, squeeze the air out of the cheeks with a "pooh" articulation. The cheek muscles squeeze the air out of the mouth in the same way that a mouthful of water can be expelled "fountain style".

To go into detail about the tongue position and embouchure used in producing this "mouth-air-only" note:

Embouchure:

1. Keep the lower lip in contact with the lip plate as much as possible. As in traditional playing, it is important to keep contact with the lip plate for its entire length, side to side. This will help to...

2. Keep the center of the embouchure stable while the corners of the lips are moving.

Tongue position:

1. The back of the tongue is raised to touch at or near the rear edge of the hard palate.

2. The front of the tongue is placed so that it touches the tips and rear surfaces of the lower teeth.

3. The center of the tongue is bowed downwards, helping to provide a large space in the mouth.

In playing the "mouth-air-only" note, the sequence of events is as follows: Start with an inflated embouchure, as outlined in exercise 2 (compression at the center of the lips). Using a "pooh" articulation to start the note, squeeze the air out of the mouth, gradually changing to a regular embouchure (compression at the corners of the lips). The back of the tongue stays in place touching the rear of the hard palate throughout. For the first phases of this practice, keep the front and center of the tongue in place also, and use only the cheek muscles to expel the air from the mouth. Again, the quality of the first note is not at all important—making a sound (and sustaining the effort) are what count. Note: At this point, use only the air stored in the mouth to produce a note, not the breath one would normally exhale from the lungs.

At first, the note will be short, perhaps only a fraction of a second. Daily practice of this exercise should be concentrated on striving to make the note longer, and to improve its quality. The first goal is to play a soft note for two to four seconds using only the air stored in the mouth. Once this has been accomplished, begin practicing throughout the flute's range. A seventh chord pattern is given below. The flutist will find that the upper notes will require a good deal of strength at the center of the embouchure, for without the support of the breath, the air must be compressed by the lips a great deal more than usual. This strength will help in traditional playing at very low dynamic levels. The low notes, specifically the first octave right hand pitches, are difficult to produce as well, but for different reasons. Firstly, these notes weakened by large-scale inflation of the cheeks due to the acoustical reason of the mouth resonating high notes well and low notes poorly when the cheeks are puffed out. Secondly, it is difficult to squeeze the air out of the cheeks slowly enough to make high quality low notes. Thus, for lower notes and as a backup for circular breathing on higher pitches, there is an alternative method to using the cheek muscles. This is using the tongue to push the air out of the mouth. This pushing method is not as efficient but helps to get things going in case of difficulty. To do this, the back of the tongue remains in contact with the hard palate at the back of the mouth, while the center of the tongue bows upward towards the roof of the mouth, but the center does not touch the roof of the mouth. The tip and front part of the tongue do the most work. In the tongue push method, the tip of the tongue is placed so that it touches the roots of the lower teeth. The cheeks are only slightly inflated and, to produce the "mouth-air-only" note, both the cheeks and tongue are used. The cheeks' squeezing action is performed, but on a reduced scale, and the tip of the tongue is moved upwards and forwards, as if to scoop up air and push it through the embouchure. As this skill is worked on, variations in the starting position of the tongue should be developed. These include placing the tongue's tip further back in the mouth, so that it is not in contact with the teeth or gums and, also, starting with the tip of the tongue placed even lower than the roots of the teeth. Both these variations serve to allow the tongue to make a larger motion, and to be more effective in its scooping action. Mixing the cheek's squeezing action with the tongue's pushing scooping action is wise, and leads to the ability to elide between these techniques depending on the pitch of the note being used when circular breathing. The tongue-push method is also the primary method used in circular breathing when playing alto and bass flutes.

Play this pattern, working to sustain the "mouth-air-only" notes. The ranges of the different methods of expelling air from the mouth are:

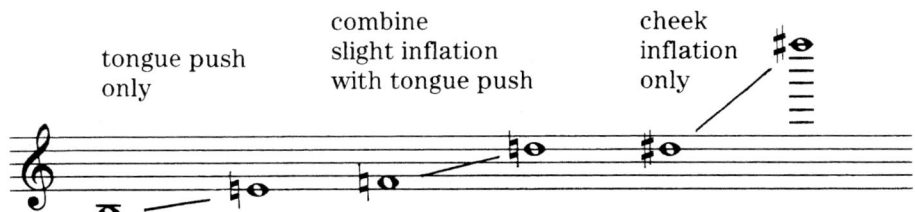

Take normal breaths as needed throughout the exercise, but play each note only with the air stored in the mouth and cheeks.

Exercise 5: **Inhaling while playing the "mouth-air-only" note:**

Once again, we'll begin without the flute. Fill the cheeks, and, while squeezing the air out, simultaneously inhale through the nose. Don't wait until the cheeks are empty to breathe. We can encounter a deeply seated habit here, i.e., throughout our careers as flutists, from the first note at the first lesson to the present moment, the sound has always stopped when air has been inhaled. This is about to change, and both the conscious and unconscious aspects of learning and habits will need to adjust. Visualize two cars in opposite lanes passing each other. Both cars begin motion at the same time; air is squeezed out of the mouth and air is inhaled through the nose simultaneously. (Naturally, one will want to breathe normally between repetitions of this exercise.)

Next, with the flute, and using the easiest note found in exercise 4, inhale while you play that note only with the air stored in the mouth. The sequence of events:

1. With the flute in playing position but the embouchure not yet formed, exhale about half of the air in the lungs. (This should lead to a feeling of needing a breath, but not uncomfortably so.)

2. Close the lips, inflate the cheeks and put the tongue in the "gonnnn" position. The mouth and cheeks now contain a reservoir of air, isolated from the breathing path of nose to lungs.

3. Simultaneously begin the two actions of squeezing the air out of the mouth (remember the "pooh" articulation) to play the "mouth-air-only" note and inhale a small amount of air through the nose.

When you look in a mirror while practicing this exercise, it will appear as if the sound and picture have gotten out of phase, and , indeed, are reversed. Practice the same seventh chord pattern as in the previous exercise, but this time, *exhale* before each note and inhale while playing each note. This will be quite a workout for the abdominal muscles, and frequent, short rest periods of about fifteen seconds are sensible. When the "mouth-air-only" note can be played for about two seconds throughout most of the flute's range, it is time to move on.

The symbol to exhale through the mouth without playing is:

The symbol to inhale through the nose while playing is:

Practice the seventh chord pattern in this manner:

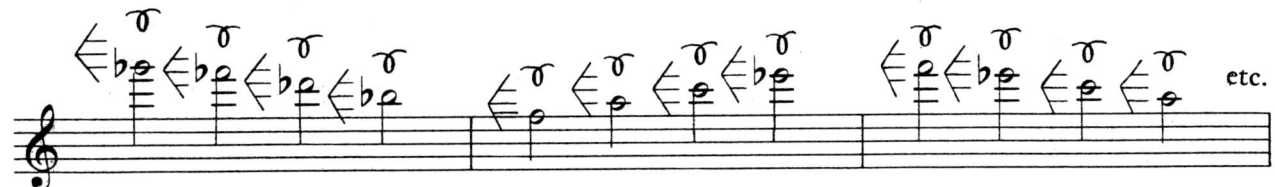

Exercise 6: **The water exercise for the coordinations needed in circular breathing**

This exercise, which involves a glass of water and a straw, is the traditional first study in circular breathing. It is sixth in this method because, for many, myself included, it is too complicated to start with. The previous exercises have dealt with the component parts of the circular breathing cycle, and now it makes sense to put those parts together.

Fill a glass halfway with water, and, exhaling through a straw, try to keep the bubbles going while circular breathing. (My first effort at this produced a remarkably bizarre misdirection of the water, which found its way into my nose.) The water provides some slight resistance, which helps, and makes the process visual. In detail, the following steps occur:

1. Exhale normally through the straw into the water. Bubbles ensue.

2. While continuing to exhale, inflate the cheeks as much possible.

3. Bring the back of the tongue into contact with the roof of the mouth at or near the back of the hard palate, and squeeze the now-isolated air stored in the cheeks and mouth out, through the straw and into the water. The bubbles should continue. Simultaneously, inhale a small amount of air through the nose.

4. As soon as the air is inhaled, drop the back of the tongue and begin to exhale normally (still through the straw). The bubbles should continue uninterruptedly.

The tongue-push method of expelling the air stored in the mouth should also be used in this practice, and some may find that this works well as the first step. Should that be the case, be sure to go on and practice expelling the air by squeezing with the cheek muscles as well.


Exercise 7: **Circular breathing on long tones**

Before beginning this phase, there is a very important point to keep in mind: circular breathing is comprised of many small inhalations taken close together. Don't wait for the physical need to breathe; it is difficult and noisy to inhale a full breath through the nostrils. And, once again, a reminder: don't wait until the air in the mouth is used before inhaling. Perform the inhalation simultaneously with the "mouth-air-only" note. This time, however, the "mouth-air-only" note becomes simply a link between normally played notes. Eventually, the

*Using the back-pressure from the water to inflate cheeks*

*Keeping the bubbles going while squeezing air out of the cheeks and simultaneously inhaling through the nose*

different phases of circular breathing will be melded together and, to the listener, become indistinguishable.

The following exercise is done starting on a high note, and uses a count of three. Execute each step at a tempo of one per second.

1. Play the note (high B or B♭ is suggested) with a full sound.

2. Inflate the cheeks.

3. Play the note with the air stored in the mouth and inhale simultaneously. As soon as a small amount of air is inhaled, drop the back of the tongue and exhale air from the lungs, using this exhalation to continue the sound. These three steps are repeated continuously without a break in the sound.

It is very possible that this phase of the learning process may present difficulties, and it may seem as if progress is not being made. The situation may well fit this description: the cheek-filling process is fine, the coordination of inhaling while playing with the air stored in the mouth and cheeks is fine, but the stored air is used up before the newly inhaled air can be brought into play. Thus, there may be a hole in the sound, followed by a bump as the next regular exhalation is rushed to the flute. This is where patience applies, as well as a secure sense that daily practice will overcome this problem. It takes time for the embouchure to become efficient enough with the stored air to create a smooth, uninterrupted flow. As the lips develop—and this may take a few weeks to six weeks or longer—the embouchure will gradually increase in efficiency until only about one half to one third of the stored air is used while inhaling. The rest of the air stored in the mouth and cheeks will be used to cushion the "new" air, and a truly continuous sound can then be created.

Let us look again at the three steps in this exercise, now with an eye to developing refinements:

1. Play the high B or B♭ loudly, openly, with the best sound possible. Use the air to support the sound, with the work area of the embouchure at the sides of the mouth and with the center somewhat relaxed.

2. Sustaining the high B or B♭ at a strong dynamic level, inflate the cheeks fully, allowing the sides of the mouth to relax, permitting the cheeks to puff out as much as possible. The work area of the embouchure is at the center.

3. First, BEGIN TO DEFLATE THE CHEEKS, THEN RAISE THE TONGUE SO THAT IT TOUCHES THE BACK OF THE HARD PALATE. This is done so that there is no drop in air speed when the tongue blocks the back of the mouth. The tongue's motion towards the hard palate should be quick and should be both in a forward and upwards direction. The tongue should move to the back of the hard palate virtually instantly after the cheek muscles firm and begin the deflation motion. The speed of this motion must be coordinated with the speed of the air. The tongue's motion should not raise or lower the pressure inside the mouth. At the moment the tongue makes contact with the hard palate, inhalation begins, and is a short, relatively shallow sniff. THE INHALATION SHOULD BE ABOUT ONE HALF OF A SECOND LONG. After inhaling, there still should be air left in the cheeks and mouth. The tongue is now lowered and the "new", next regular exhalation is started. The tongue motion, however, should be refined so that it is not a simple dropping down

motion, but rather is a smooth motion both forward and down. This permits the "new air" to be mixed with the air remaining in the cheeks and mouth. Aurèle Nicolet likens the motion of the tongue moving away from the hard palate as similar to "a wave rolling onto a beach". Indeed, the tongue may first move forward, staying in contact with the hard palate, before beginning to be lowered. This is done to keep the air speed constant at the embouchure, and to gradually open the pathway for the normally exhaled air. This elision between playing with the air stored in the cheeks and the "new" air exhaled normally, is the key to success in the "restarting" process, the most difficult phase of circular breathing. AFTER INHALING, DO NOT RELAX THE CHEEKS IMMEDIATELY. Continue the deflating motion of the cheeks as the new, normally exhaled air enters the mouth. USE A COMBINATION OF THE CHEEK MUSCLES SQUEEZING ACTION AND A QUICK, BUT SMOOTH "CRESCENDO" IN THE NORMALLY EXHALED AIR TO KEEP THE AIR PRESSURE AND SPEED AT THE FRONT OF THE MOUTH CONSTANT. This mixing process permits the new breath to be added gradually, over a period of about one-half of a second. Over time, as practice leads to skill and confidence, the inhalation period should be reduced to one-third of a second, and the "restarting" elision should be lengthened to some two-thirds of a second. After the change-over between the stored air and the following normally exhaled air, continue the deflation motion (if it is not complete), re-establish the normal embouchure, and, while still holding the note, prepare to begin the inflation process, and thus the entire cycle, anew.

Practice long tones with ten circular breaths per note. Take a short rest after each long tone, and use the time to analyze what was successful, and what wasn't. Play at least fifteen of these long tones per practice session. Examples of this follow:

The symbol for inflating the cheeks while playing is:

This links up with the symbol to inhale through the nose while playing:

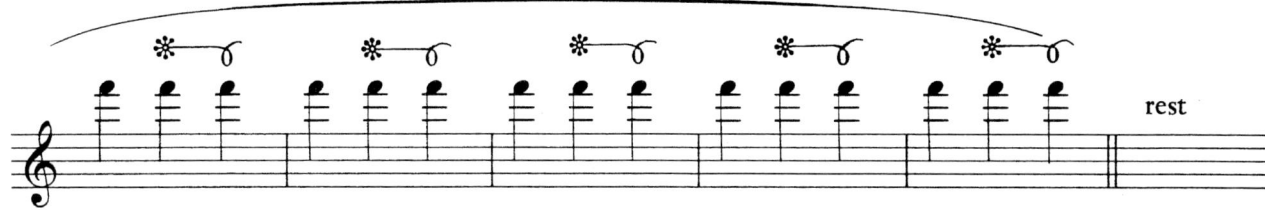

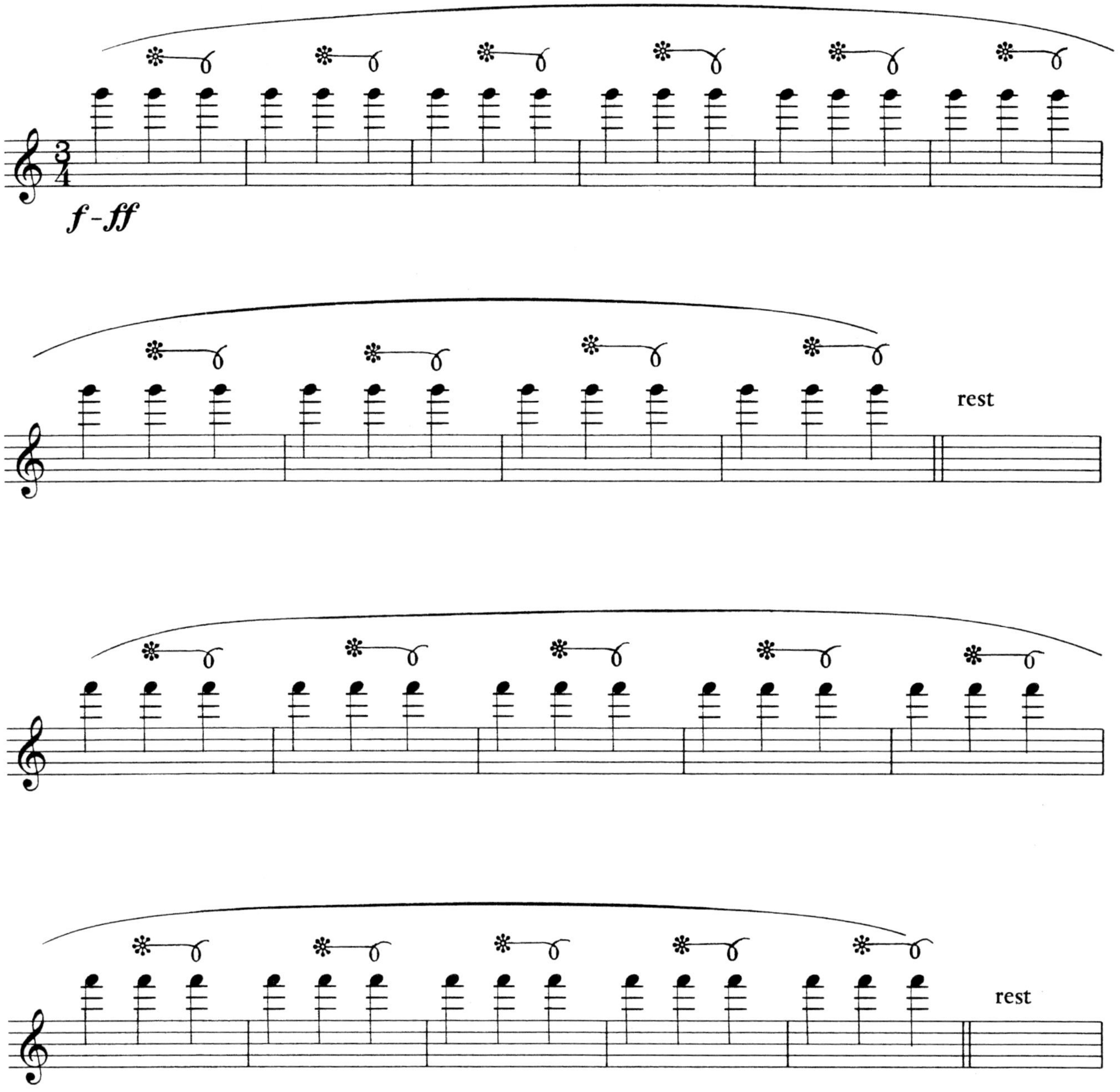

*The cheeks inflated and deflated. Note how the sides of the embouchure move and the center remains stable throughout the sequence.*

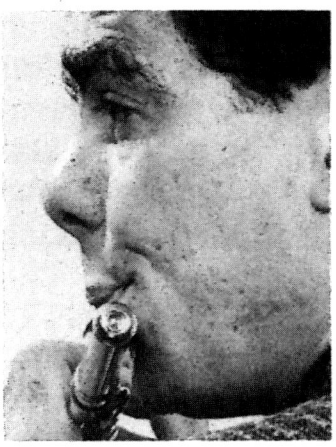

*Cycle begins with regular embouchure*

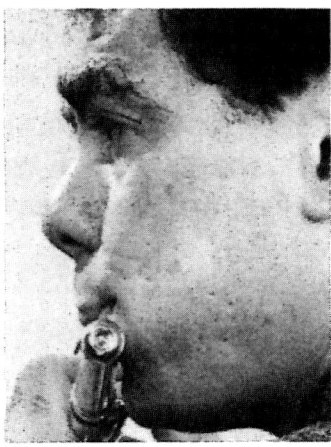

*Inflation begins*

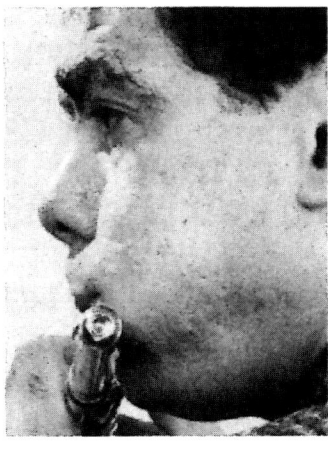

*Inflation continues*

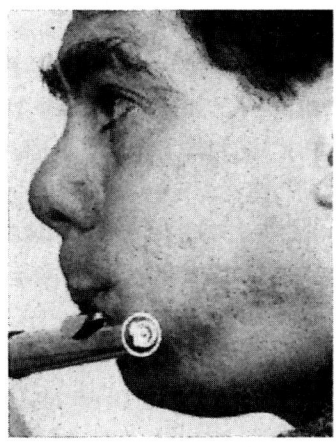

*Inflation is complete and inhalation begins*

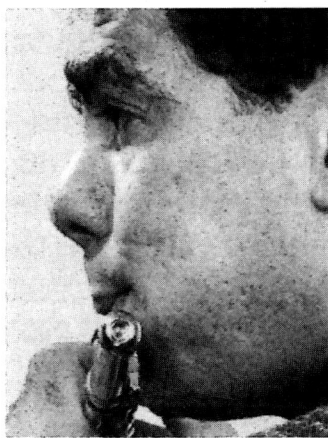

*Inhalation complete, air from lungs is "restarted" while deflation continues*

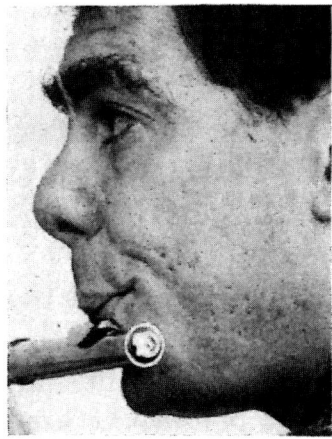

*The cycle begins anew with regular embouchure*

# CHAPTER II

# INTERMEDIATE PHASES

After the basic mechanics of circular breathing have become functional—even with bumps, thin spots and jumps in the sound—practicing the technique in scale patterns and other traditional daily studies should begin. Frequent, shallow breaths will be the order of the day, and refining the nasal inhalation so that it is not noisy is one of the next tasks on the agenda. Also, becoming aware of, and beginning to control, the large-scale inhalations and exhalations that take place over many small breaths is to be taken up.

To begin, continue pactice of the long tones, but now add such scale patterns as that found in Tafannel and Gaubert's *Seventeen Daily Exercises* as #4. Play this study *forte*, all *legato* at ♩=50-60, and take a circular breath every four eighth notes. At first, keep going even when there are holes in the sound and obvious pitch changes. After a week or two, repeat any measure that had such imperfections, and keep repeating those measures until an improvement (not to the point of perfection, but to an audible degree) is heard. Practice with two patterns of breathing: first with the breath (inhalation) in the last of each group of four notes, then with the breath on the first note of each group. Although the pattern begins with C major in Tafannel and Gaubert, starting on F major is somewhat easier. Assuming for the moment that the breath will be taken during The fourth eighth note, the following sequence occurs:

1. During the first eighth note the embouchure is in its normal mode for the pitch being played.

2. Inflate the cheeks during the second and third eighths, and, if possible, flare the nostrils during the third eighth note. This opens wider passages for the inhalation and helps reduce noise.

3. Take a circular breath during the fourth eighth note. Depending on the pitch of the note, a choice will have been made about using the cheeks or the tongue, or a combination, to expel the air from the mouth. USE THE ENTIRE LENGTH OF THE FOURTH EIGHTH NOTE TO INHALE. IF POSSIBLE, DO NOT DEFLATE CHEEKS COMPLETELY WHILE INHALING.

4. Drop the tongue to reopen the normal exhalation path on the beginning of the first eighth note of the next group. If any air remained in the cheeks after inhaling, continue to squeeze with the cheek muscles, using this bellows action to help keep the speed of the airstream constant at the embouchure.

Examples of both placements of the inhalation follow:

At this point, two problems are likely to be making themselves felt. The inhalation is likely to be noisy, at least some of the time, and the release, the dropping motion of the tongue may well be causing an unevenness in the sound. This unevenness may be anything from a slight accent to a marked change in quality. To deal with the nasal inhalation first, there are several approaches to this problem that will be helpful:

1. Practice sniffing. Spend thirty seconds to a minute daily doing a panting exercise, but breathe through the nose, with the mouth closed. This should help strengthen the abdominal muscles, which have to pull air through the nostrils.

2. Make sure the chest wall (front of the chest) is raised BEFORE BREATHING. This puts you in a position where it is mechanicaly easier to inhale (also true for regular inhalations). With the chest wall raised, use the abdominal muscles to pull air into your lungs. Since the chest wall will already be in the right position for inhaling, no muscular energy will be needed to move the rib cage while breathing, just the air.

3. If you can do it, be sure to flare the nostrils before inhaling. Like curling the tongue, this seems to be the sort of thing that not everyone can do. If you can't, don't worry about it; its not that important. If you can, don't forget about it; every little bit helps.

4. While inhaling, have the feeling of pushing the voice box downwards, this will open the trachea to its widest diameter, therefore its least resistant shape. (This is also extremely important in regular breathing.)

5. Make sure you are circular breathing frequently. If you wait until you need air, you will be placing yourself in a very difficult situation. It is quite hard to take in a full breath through the nostrils. Doing so is certain to create a clearly audible sniffing or, even worse, snorting sound that is disruptive to the musical flow. Remember, when circular breathing, to breathe early and often.

The release of the tongue is another area where concentrated work will help result in approaching smooth, seamless results. At first, a bump in the sound is acceptable. As time passes, this aspect of circular breathing, while still detectable, should be like an exceptional bow change, quiet, appearing to be effortless. The following observations will help you reach this level. Eventually, the tongue drop will be perfectly, absolutely inaudible.

1. Matching the speed of the "new" air with the speed of the air being squeezed out of the mouth is important. Thus, when the tongue is

lowered, there will not be a sudden jump in the volume of the tone. It may be necessary to take shallower nasal inhalations, taking less time and therefore leaving more air stored in the mouth at the moment the tongue is lowered.

2. The motion of the tongue should first be forward along the roof of the mouth. As the back of the tongue is moved forward to the point where the roof of the mouth begins to arch upwards steeply, there will be a natural opening of the pathway as the tongue continues to move forward.

3. At the moment when the tongue is to be lowered, try to make this a "peeling" motion, thus separating the back of the tongue from the roof of the mouth in a fashion more gradual than sudden. To make this motion, lower the top surface of the tongue from the front towards the back. This "top surface", of course, refers only to the area of the tongue that makes contact with the hard palate.

4. Try to avoid exclusive use of the tongue-push method of expelling air from the mouth. Even on very soft or very low notes, the slightest bit of cheek inflation helps reduce the chance of a bump in the sound when the tongue is lowered. When the tongue-push method is used without any cheek inflation, it is extremely difficult to prevent a thinning of the sound followed by the aforementioned bump.

As you practice scale studies with circular breathing, the frequency of noisy nasal inhalations will gradually decrease, as will the frequency and degree of changes in the quality and volume of the sound. At this point, it may well be possible to keep the lungs virtually fully inflated all the time. With the frequent inhalations, it becomes possible to constantly inhale as much or more air than was exhaled in each circular breath cycle. When I discovered this phenomenon, I thought that it might be a good thing, as it would enable the chest to act as a resonator constantly at its full size. I soon learned that keeping the lungs fully inflated leads to discomfort. The lungs are in their natural state when they are constantly inflating and deflating, and the body resists holding these tissues in one position for very long. Thus, it became necessary to design a strategy for long-term circular breathing that works well both musically and physiologically. The answer is to make a gradual inhalation over a number of circular breath inhalations, i.e., to inhale more air than is exhaled in each circular breath cycle for some six to ten times. This is followed by a long-term exhalation, in which less air is inhaled than is exhaled in each circular breath cycle for a similar number of times. This leads to a sensation of "puffing up" gradually, then "puffing down". At first, there is little chance that circular breathing will be efficient enough to cause this problem, but by this phase, the long-term inhalations and exhalations should be given attention. It will make practice less fatiguing.

After some weeks of work on scale studies, it will begin to be obvious that breathing every four eighth notes is no longer necessary. Change to inhaling once in every eight note group. Also, work on breathing more frequently when making the long-term inhalation, and inhaling less frequently when producing the long-term exhalation. Examples follow:

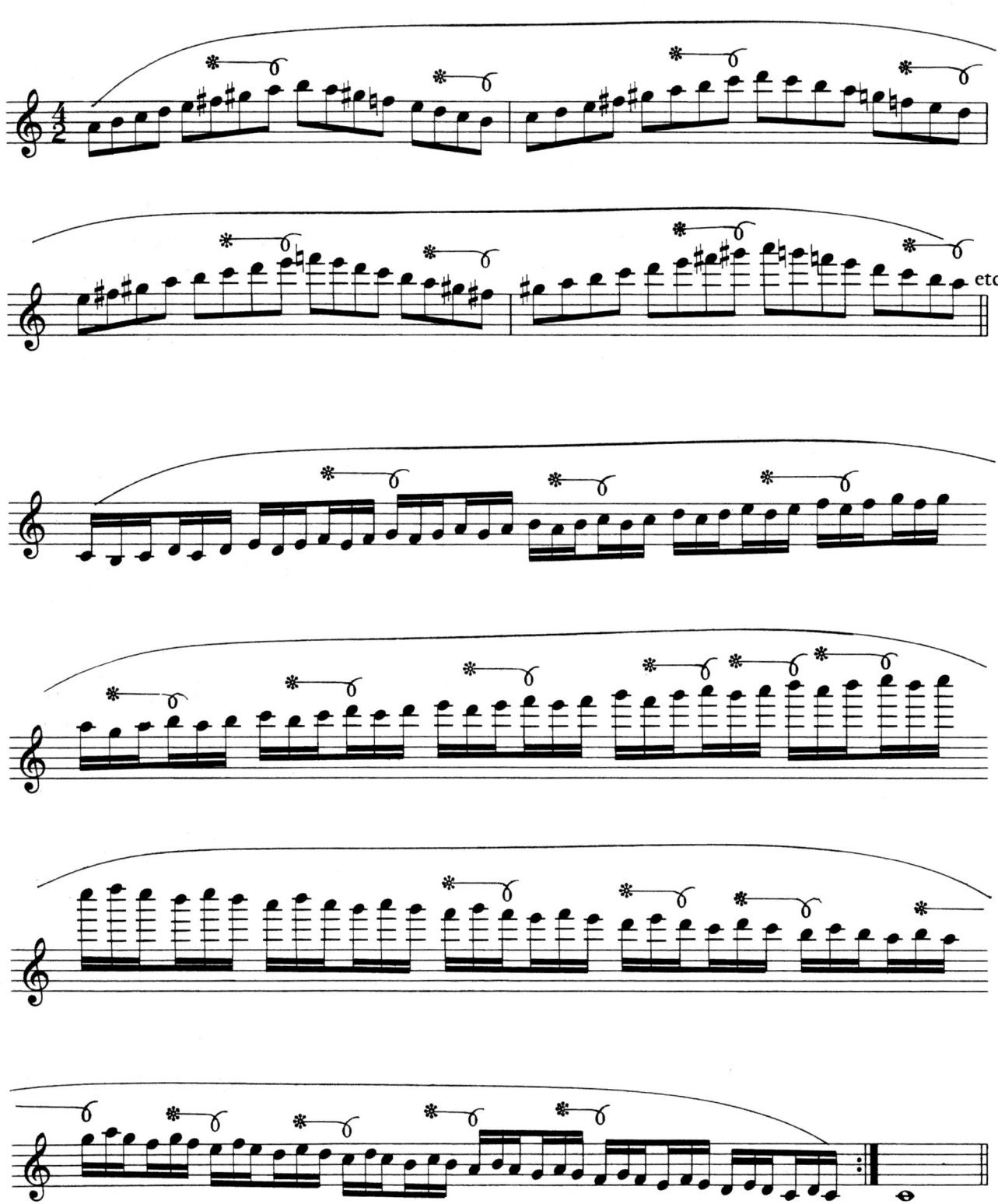

Since music rarely confines itself to neat, four and eight note groups in scale patterns, we should now turn attention to finding optimal placements for circular breaths in musical situations. The examples that follow are drawn from the etude repertoire, as I feel that the concert repertoire should not be used until these skills are more developed. In deciding how to best place the circular breaths, one must first survey the line to be played (not often enough done when regular breaths are to be used). A few basic guidelines are helpful—but each of these rules has exceptions, and, although the examples are from etudes, the work being done is to prepare for musical expression in pieces. Thus, in case of doubt, do what you feel will be best musically.

1. Runs and trills are optimal places for circular breathing. Indeed, the trill is the perfect spot to begin, as the rapidly alternating notes can be very effective in covering imperfections in circular breathing. Not surprisingly, my first public effort with circular breathing was carefully placed in a trill. Likewise, the pitch changes in runs aid in disguising flaws. There are several ways to place circular breaths into trills and runs. Best is if there is time to include the entire cycle—inflation, inhalation/deflation, restarting—within the trill or run. If the musical gesture is not long enough for this, it is best to inflate the cheeks before hand.

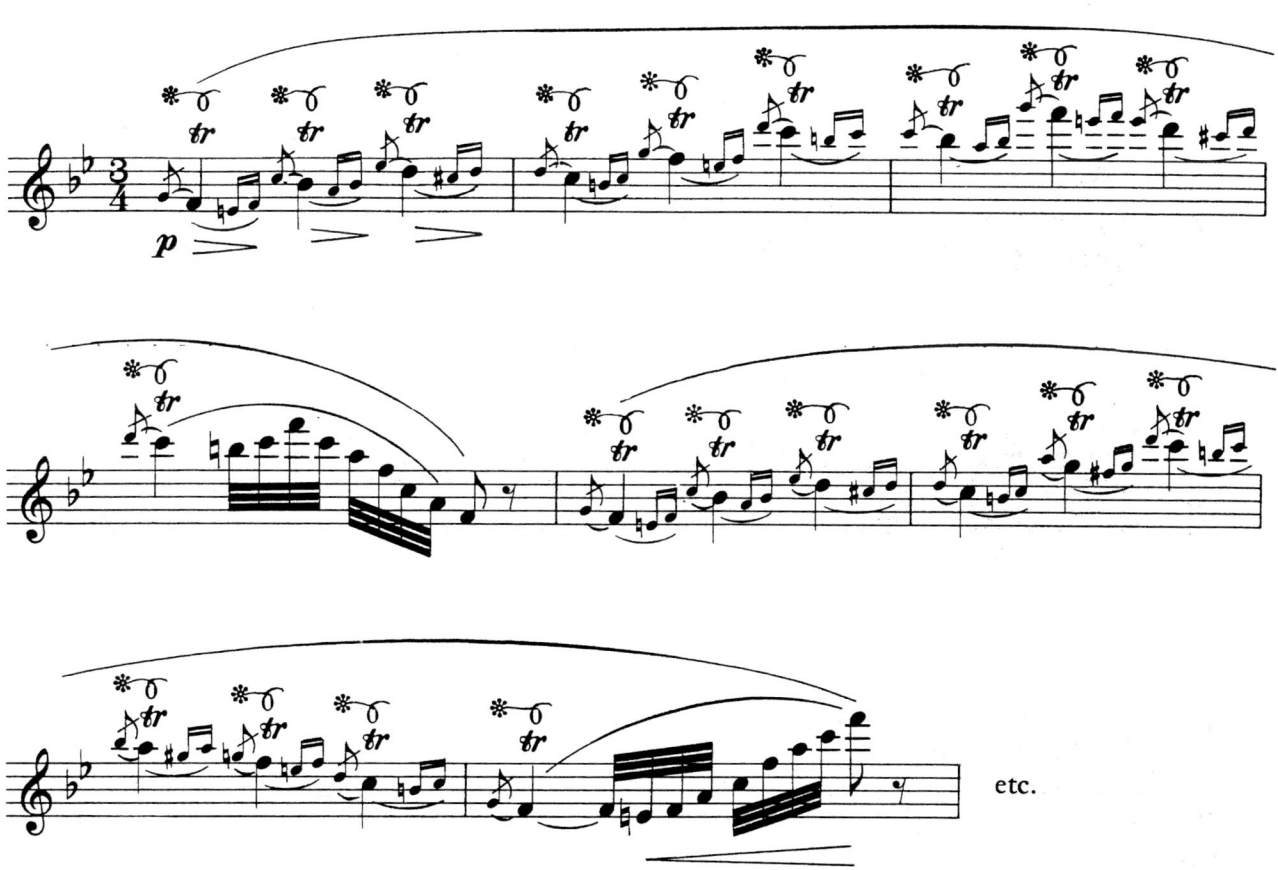

2. Look for the high point(s) in the pitch contour of phrases. It is easier to circular breathe on higher notes. Inflate the cheeks when approaching the high point in the line, and, depending on the musical content, inhale either close to, at, or after the highest note.

3. In music with repeated patterns or sequences, use the musically least important element of the repeating pattern to circular breathe. Regardless of the breathing method used, these places would be played more softly than the more important elements, and the dynamic should be the same when circular breathing is used.

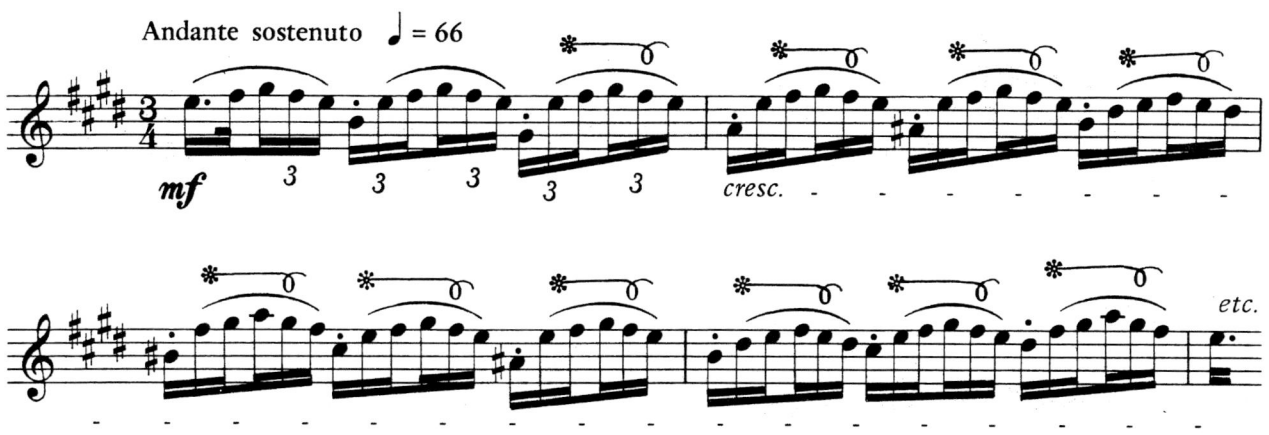

First for endurance, then for seamlessness and musical integration, practice entire etudes with circular breathing. Many etudes suggest themselves as appropriate vehicles for this, and many others are easily adapted. Any study marked with long slurs throughout (such as Anderson's Opus 15, #10 in C# minor), or marked with frequent *legato* passages (as in Anderson's famous Opus 15, #3 in G major or Boehm's Opus 26, #21 in D major and #24 in E minor) will be effective. The etudes can be practiced all *legato* with the written articulations removed, and as written. I recommend that practice be concentrated on the etudes with their articulations included. This is the best preparation for working on actual pieces both from the technical and the aesthetic point of view. For long-term exercising of the mechanics, and only the mechanics, of circular breathing, daily studies such as Tafannel and Gaubert are a better choice than etudes played without articulations. Superlong long tones of three to five minutes are also useful exercises for the purely technical aspects.

Suggested etudes include:

Anderson: Opus 21 — #2 A minor
#6 B minor
#11 B major
#14 E♭ minor
#16 B♭ minor
#19 E♭ major
#20 C minor
#21 B♭ major
#22 G minor
#23 F major
#24 D minor

Opus 15 — #1 C major
#3 G major
#4 E minor
#5 D major
#7 A major
#8 F# minor
#10 C# minor
#11 B major
#13 F# major
#14 D#/E♭ minor
#15 D♭ major
#19 E♭ major
#21 B♭ major
#23 F major

Opus 33 — #1 C major
#3 G major
#4 E minor
#5 D major
#7 A major
#8 F# minor
#9 E major
#12 G# minor
#14 D# minor
#17 A♭ major
#24 D minor

Boehm: Opus 26 — #1 C major
#2 A minor
#3 F major
#4 D minor
#5 B♭ major
#7 E♭ major
#8 C minor
#9 A♭ major
#11 D♭ major
#12 B minor
#13 F# major
#14 E♭ minor
#17 E major
#18 C# minor
#19 A major
#21 D major
#22 B minor
#23 G major
#24 E minor

# CHAPTER III

# CIRCULAR BREATHING IN ORCHESTRAL, RECITAL & CONCERTO REPERTOIRE

When applying circular breathing to repertoire, aesthetic as well as technical considerations must be made. In themselves, any and all techniques are meaninglesss, they are but means to the end of musical expression. Therefore, when thinking of using circular breathing in a piece not specifically calling for this technique, the burning question is: **Can I better express the musical content with circular breathing?** I believe the answer to this question is "yes" on very many occasions, but sometimes the answer is "no". I don't feel, for example, that circular breathing through the *Allemande* of J.S. Bach's A minor *Partita* is a musically desirable choice. Pieces that need to breathe must be allowed to breathe, or they smother. Interestingly, use of circular breathing in the *Sarabande* of Bach's *Partita* can be very helpful and very expressive. It is most natural that, having invested a great deal of time, work and heart to learn this technique, there is a strong desire to use circular breathing, and there are plenty of musically valid places for this. Now, with the aesthetic message clear, it is at last time to turn to repertoire.

In the orchestra, circular breathing is useful, especially in solo passages in which the dynamic markings are not to be played as written, but to be played so that the audience hears them at the written dynamics. The solo flutist often must play at well above the written dynamics so that the sound carries over the (not always sensitive) rest of the orchestra. This requires a good deal more air than usual, and can turn a phrase that is easy in practice into a challenge of an entirely greater technical magnitude. As a first example, the solo from Berlioz's *L'Enfance du Christ* has perfectly placed spots for circular breathing. Each of the first three measures has a moving figure ideal for a circular breath, and the *tessitura* is not problematic.

Be sure to include the first of each group of four thirty-second notes in the inflation phase. Bring the tongue up and circular breathe during the second and third note of each group. By restarting on the fourth thirty-second, a very smooth transition can be made. Should the transitions into and out of the circular breathing not be perfect, the note movement will help disguise this.

Beethoven's *Leonore Overture No. 3* presents somewhat more involved challenges. Right at the outset of the piece, there is a strong chord followed by a *diminuendo* and a slow, exposed scale downwards for the first flutist. Some conductors like this passage, marked as *adagio*, to be dramatically slow. A good strategy is to take a deep regular breath before starting, and to supplement this with a circular breath within the first measure. Take the circular breath before the dynamic drops very far, and play the rest of the passage without further inhalations. This allows you to play the exposed measures starting with full reserves of air.

Later in this work, the flutist plays the famous solo and, at its end, is far from done. There are still just over eight measures to go holding the third octave D♮! A circular breath early in this held note will turn this moment from difficult to easy, and will free the flutist from having to insert "extra" breaths into the solo to build up reserves for holding the D♮.

In Paul Hindemith's *Symphonic Metamorphoses*, there is a flute solo that presents breathing problems because of its speed. In his *20th Century Orchestra Studies*, John Krell recommends that the second flutist cover short sections of the solo while the first flutist breathes. Another approach is circular breathing, taking frequent, small inhalations in a few, critical places. This example picks up the solo at rehearsal letter C:

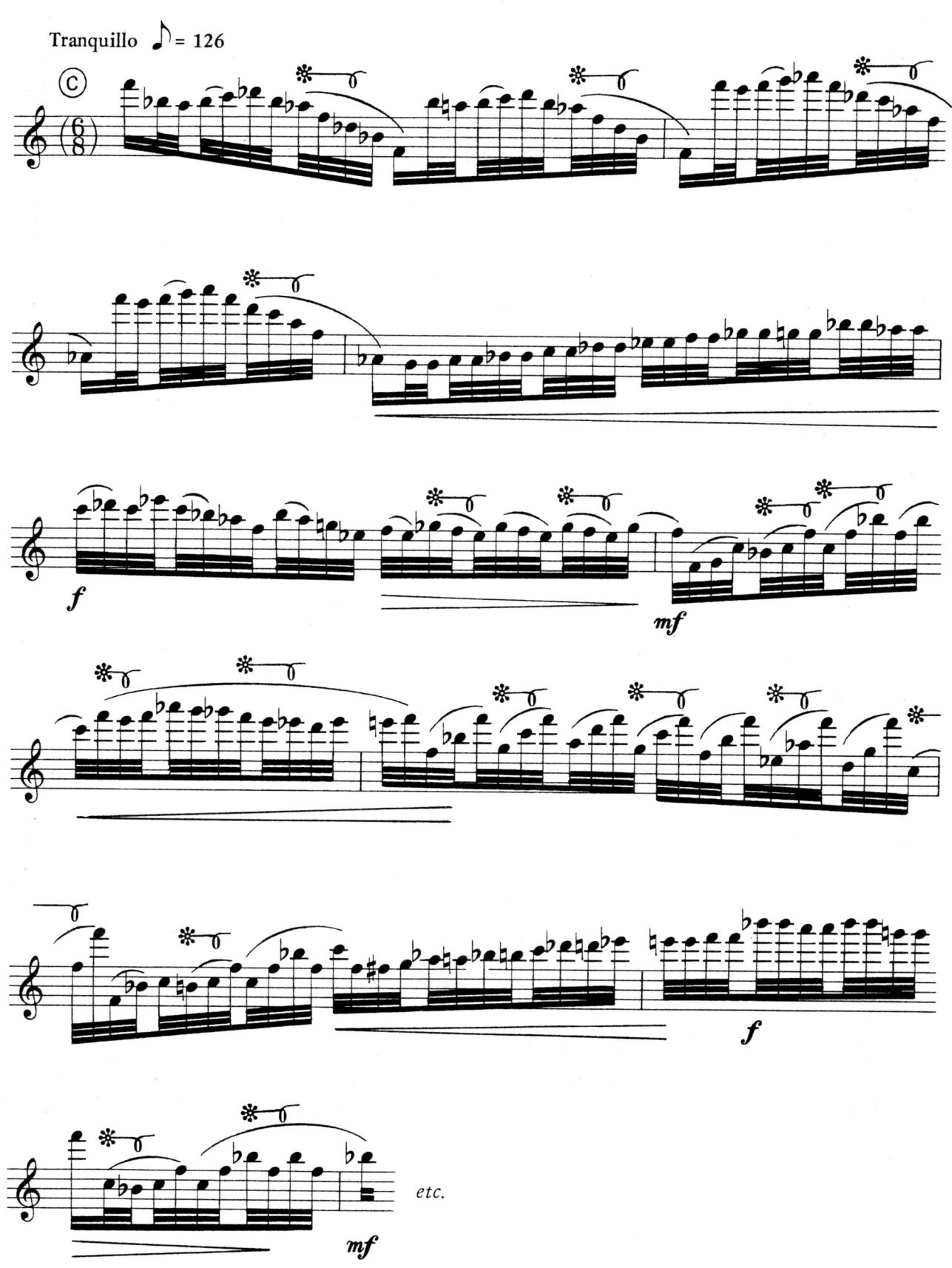

The major solo in Ravel's *Daphnis et Chloé Suite #2* is one of the greatest and most difficult statements for the orchestral flutist. It is marked *tres lent, expressif et souple*, but, due to the length of the phrases and the power needed to project over the accompaniment, this solo (to my ears, at least), is often performed too quickly and/or without enough expressive subtlety. With circular breathing, dynamics can be more freely handled and the tempo slowed. Circular breathing in this solo, however, must be performed at the highest level. Any pitch fluctuations will be clearly heard, and the circular breath inhalations often must be placed on the difficult third octave E, F♯ and G♯. Practice this solo with several different placements of the circular breaths. This will develop the flexibility and confidence needed to use circular breathing in this high-pressure situation.

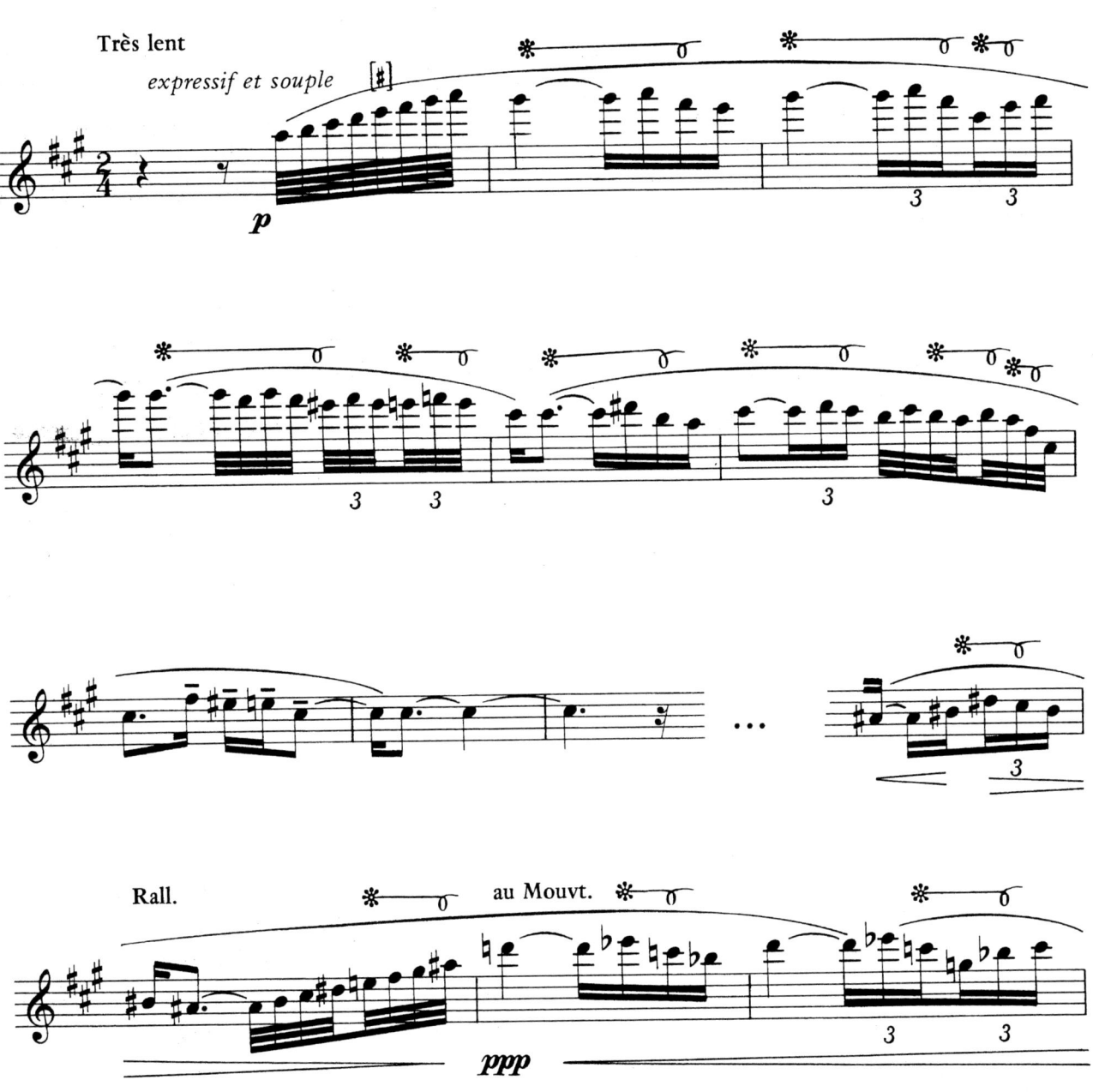

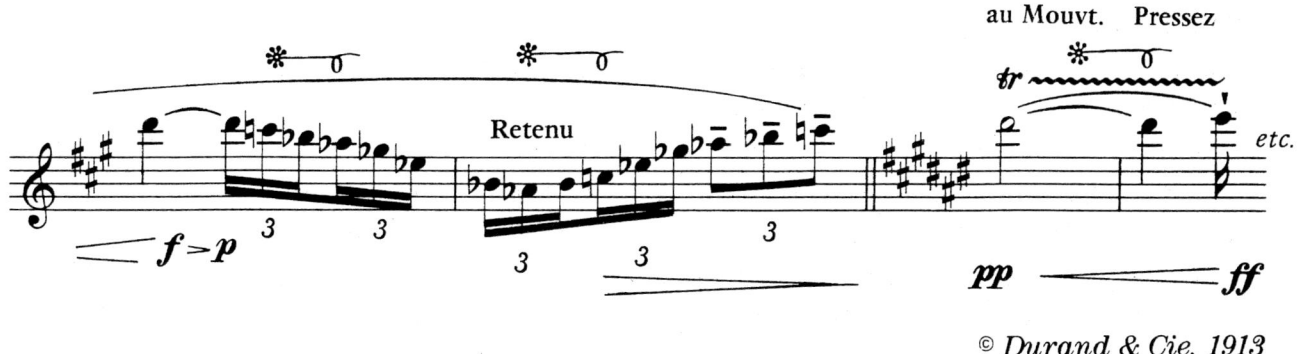

© *Durand & Cie. 1913*

Last among the orchestral examples is by far the hardest, the solo from Debussy's *L'Après-midi d'un Faune*. This phrase requires perfect matching of air speeds between the mouth-air-only exhalations and the normal exhalations that follow. Further, it may be necessary to use a very sophisticated, but delicate technique—starting the B♮ in the third measure with normal exhalation and finishing that same note with a circular breath exhalation. The elision between the two types of exhalation in a completely exposed position represents a technical challenge at the highest level. Success in meeting such challenges can open musical doors, and the results can be thrilling.

In recital repertoire, circular breathing is applicable to all styles and periods. Once again, wise aesthetic and technical decisions are necessary. To begin, three examples from the work of J.S. Bach will be considered. In applying circular breathing to Bach's music, the goal is not to produce a stunning technical effect, but to enable the difficult (sometimes very difficult) passagework to be performed with grace and freedom. A representative passage, from the *Andante* of the B minor *Sonata*, follows. By circular breathing, a regular inhalation which often disrupts the rhythmic flow can be avoided. Be sure to begin inflating the cheeks at least four sixteenth-note triplets before inhaling.

In performance, phrases that can be played in one breath in practice can become more difficult. Having circular breathing as a backup technique can be invaluable at such moments. The opening phrase of the *Adagio* in the C major *Sonata* exemplifies this. While choice of breathing placement is highly subjective, and there are several possibilities for breathing in this opening, a breath after the first sixteenth of the third measure seems optimal to me. Using this as the placement for the first regular inhalation, anything less than a well-drawn breath before starting and effective, balanced use of the air in the phrase will cause problems in getting to this chosen breath place. Should something interfere with this, a circular breath during the trill in the second measure will supplement the available air, and enable the player to complete the phrase as planned. While circular breathing is technically easy in placements such as this, practice is recommended to prepare for this type of improvisatory change in performance.

When taking repeats in the Bach *Sonatas* or other Baroque works, it is important to differentiate between the first and second playings of each repeated section. Changing phrasing to explicate different musical possibilities inherent in the score is a necessity, and an important part of this is changing breath placements. In the *Sarabande* of the A minor *Partita*, the ending of the first section can be effectively expanded on the repeat via several circular breath inhalations in the fourth and third measure before the double bar.

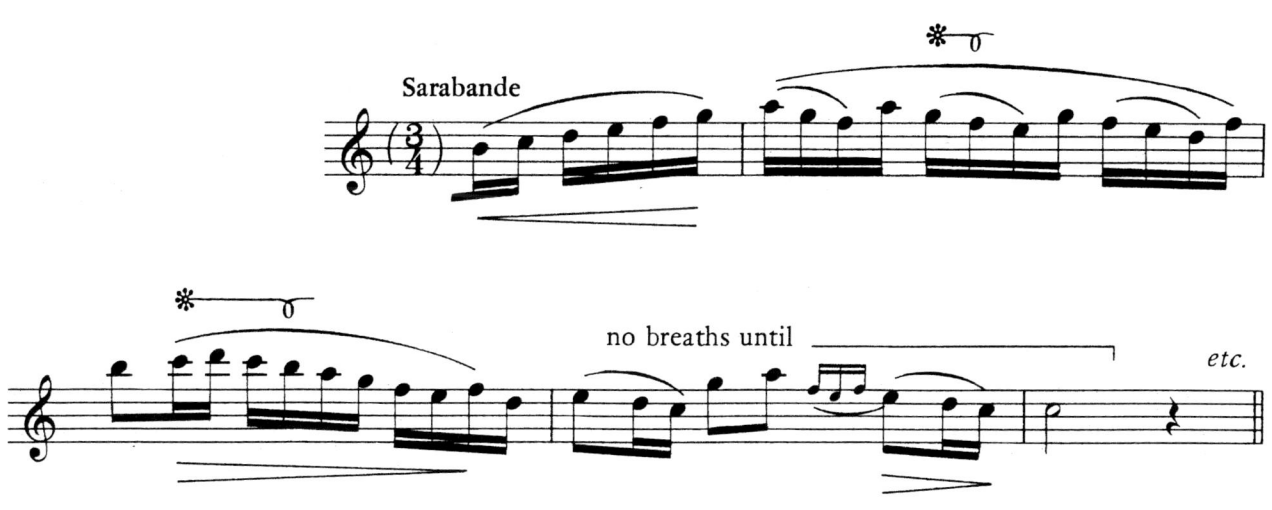

In Schubert's well-known *Introduction und Variationen Über Ihr Blümlein alle*, circular breathing can be used to solve at least two rather different musical problems. In the *Introduction*, the final phrase is quite long, and some editors have broken it down into shorter units. The poetic nature of this long, arching, aching phrase can be disrupted by inserting breaths, and circular breathing is the logical, artistic answer to the technical problem here. (In the introduction to this book, I referred to nineteenth-century Boehm flutes, and how they require less air than do modern instruments. When I played this phrase on a Boehm and Mendler flute, with its pure, small sound, the length presented no problem at all, and felt very natural.)

Later in the work, in the fifth variation, an altogether different type of breathing problem occurs—none of the phrases are very long, but in the major section of the variaion, time to breathe is minimal. Often, breaths in this section are hasty, and put the performer in a rhythmic "catch-up" situation as time lost while breathing must be regained. Circular breathing here is really quite easy; the constant, rapid scale passages are perfect for embedding circular breath inhalations. Thus, attention may be turned to the other technical problems that must be overcome before this variation can be truly balletic.

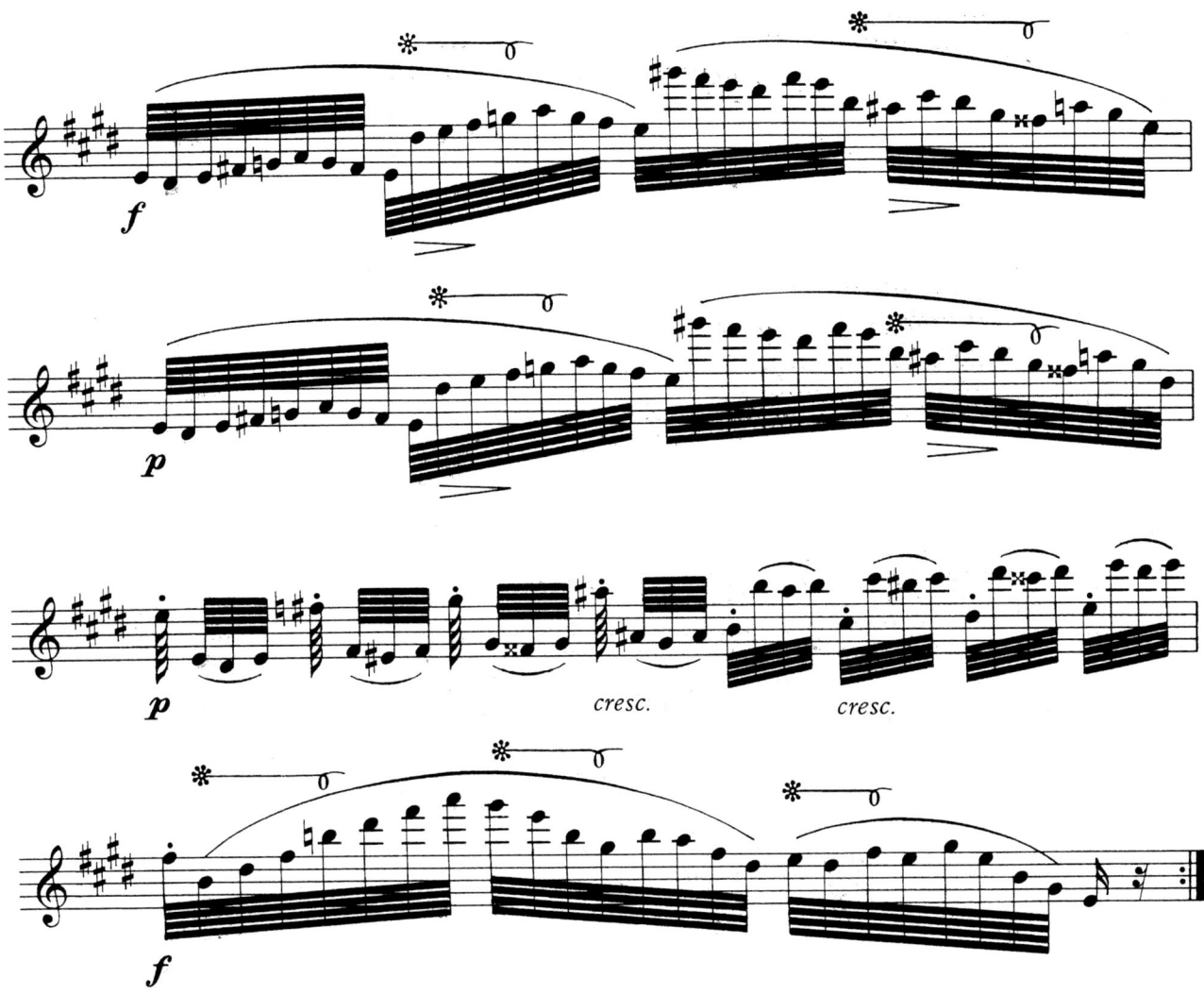

Edgard Varèse's *Density 21.5* is one of the twentieth century's seminal compositions. After a half-century, it is finally becoming widely understood as an impassioned, vibrant statement that is not at all to be played in a detached, removed manner. Varèse apparently expressed a wish that the flutist's breath could be longer at the end of the piece, and it certainly does feel musically and dramatically correct to make a *rallentando* through the last two phrases. Circular breathing is not very difficult here, but can make all the difference in extending the *crescendo* to make a truly exciting ending.

© *Assigned to Colfranc Music Publishing Corp. 1966*

*Concerti* present their own special musical joys and challenges. In the traditional soloist-protagonist role, the flutist must transcend the technical difficulties and perform with passion, flair and command. In the three *concerti* considered here, circular breathing is used both for poetic and dramatic purposes. Mozart's *Concerto II* in D major provides the first examples.

The very opening phrase of this piece, with its four measures of held D♮, is perfect for circular breathing. This makes it possible to omit an interruptive breath after the hold, and to approach dynamic changes within the hold with a more expansive approach.

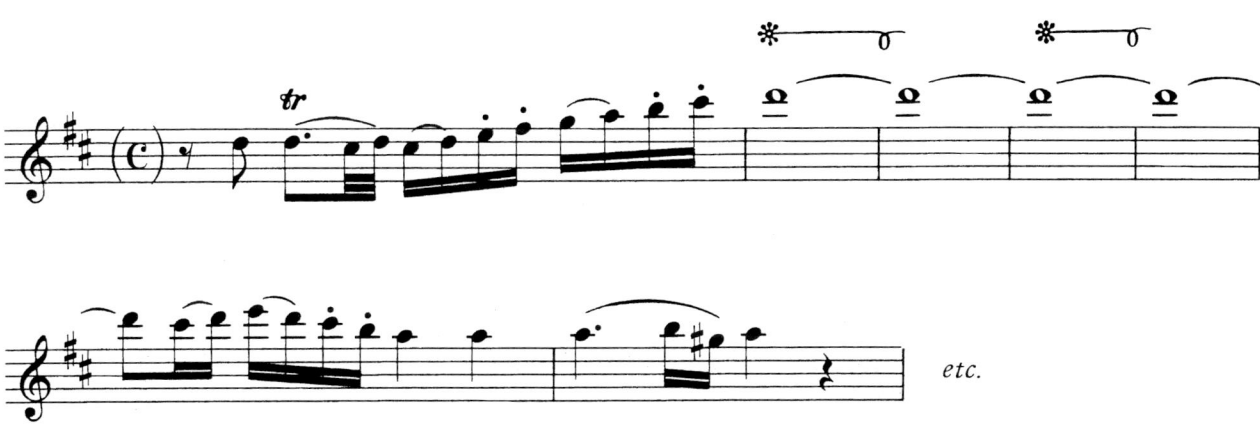

In the *andante,* circular breathing can make it possible to extend a phrase past several usual breaths:

In Cecile Chaminade's *Concertino*, circular breathing can be used for a more fiery effect. The climax of the opening statement can be made even more exciting if circular breath inhalations are taken during the upward part of the run and in the triplet figures of the melodic statement that follows. The high *tessitura* and *fortissimo* dynamic present an optimal situation for circular breathing.

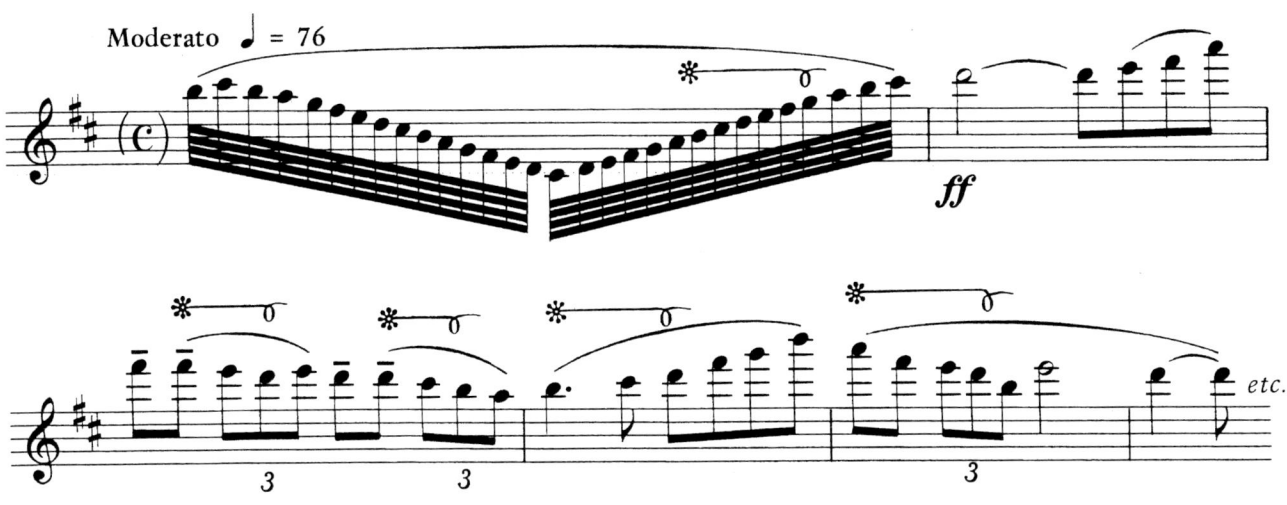

Later in the same work, the ending of the cadenza becomes more effective if circular breathing is used to avoid breathing before the trill and to make a seamless rendering of the theme over the next four measures.

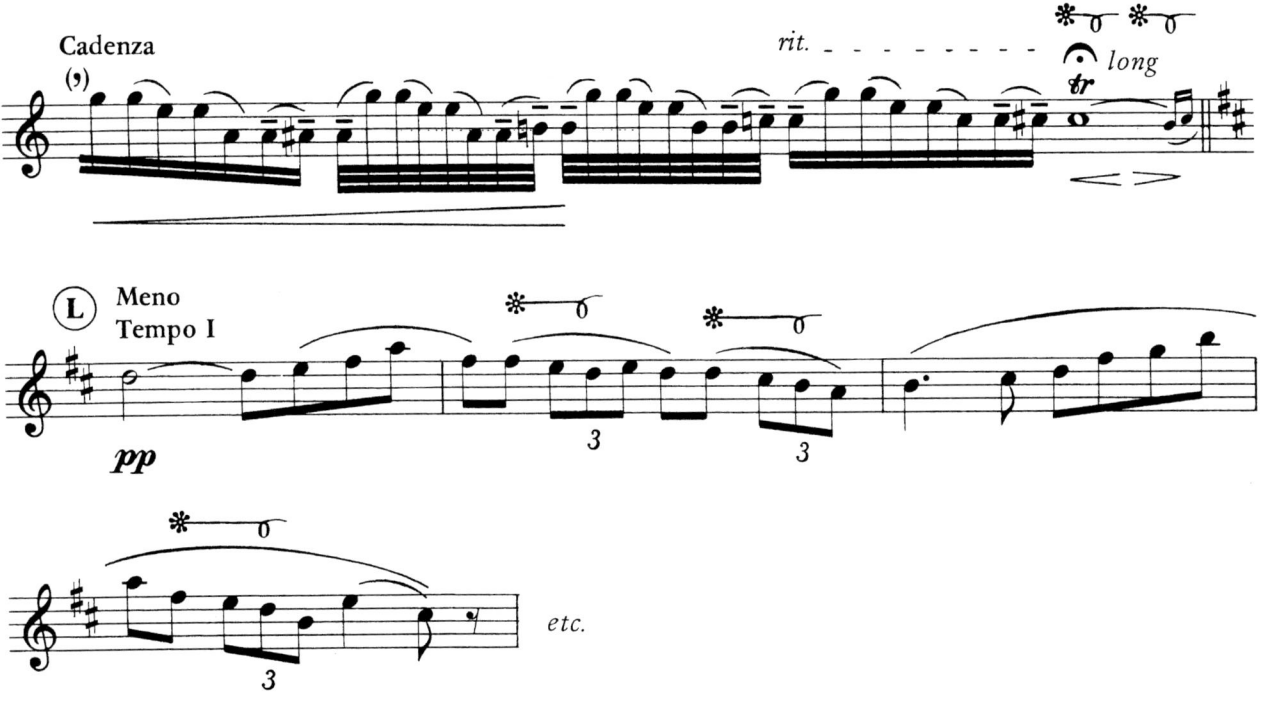

In Charles Griffes' *Poem*, an effective use of circular breathing is made in the runs and trill passagework before letter H. In the edition prepared by Georges Barrère, a rest, inserted for breathing purposes by the composer, was removed. In dramatic terms, Barrère was certainly correct, and, since he and Griffes worked together fine-tuning the piece, I feel that the change is legitimate. This doesn't make performing the work any easier, however, and use of circular breathing enables us to realize this larger vision.

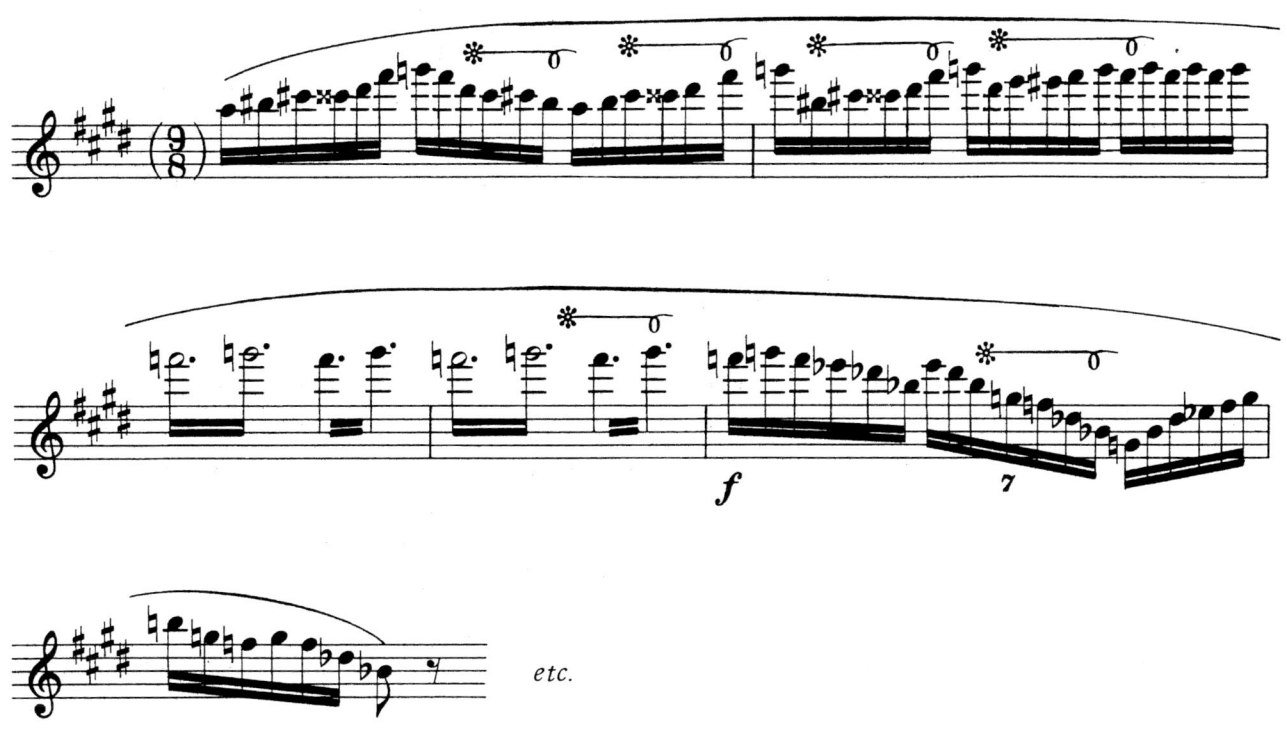

© *G. Schirmer, Inc. 1922*

The various examples in this chapter are presented to show how each performer can integrate circular breathing into his or her technique and interpretations. Technique makes expressive freedom possible, and I hope that the examples will inspire creative solutions to technical and musical problems in other works.

## Chapter IV

## ADVANCED TECHNIQUE
## CIRCULAR BREATHING IN ARTICULATIONS
## AND IN EXTENDED TECHNIQUES

This chapter presents techniques for circular breathing while single and double-tonguing, and while playing multiphonics and whispertones. While these techniques are unquestionably difficult, the flutist who has reached this point will be ready to work on them. I was first motivated to learn circular breathing so that I could create pieces with very long phrases, phrases that were natural in length for the complex multiphonic textures I was working with both as composer and performer. Extended techniques are the continued growth and development of instrumental music, and this is the expressive realm that most holds my attention and passion. As time passes, the aspects of flute technique now referred to as "extended" will become part of the mainstream.

In developing the ability to circular breathe while articulating, single tonguing should be worked on first. While slowly playing a scale or *arpeggio* pattern with the notes played quite short and well separated, slightly inflate the cheeks between two pitches. Then, with a "pooh" articulation, play the next note only with the air in the mouth, but—unlike the "mouth-air-only" notes of the first chapter—the quality of the notes must be matched to the regularly tongued notes. Use the tongue as well as the cheeks to expell the air from the mouth. Second octave pitches seem to be best for this, and they should be practiced first, but this technique must be developed throughout the flute's range.

Be sure to firm the lips at the aperture before the "pooh" articulation, and to quickly thrust the tongue forwards to match the rapid airspeed of the regular *staccato* notes. Again, use only a very slight cheek inflation if at all, and use up the air in the mouth while inhaling. Since the "restart" will be in the form of the next articulated note, there is no need to be concerned with melding into the "restart". With practice, the "pooh" articulation can be effectively made to match the regular, single tonguing.

To circular breathe while double-tonguing, substitute a "pooh" articulated note for a "tu" articulated note, and inhale while playing the "air-in-mouth" note. The "restart" will be the following "ku" articulated pitch. Practice the same type pattern as used for single tonguing, but double-tongue each pitch. Inhaling during the length of one note only works at slower speeds, of course, and to perform the high-speed tonguing that typifies flute repertorie while circular breathing requires further technical refinement. To do this, some slight cheek inflation is helpful, for two notes will be played with the stored air while inhaling. A step-by-step description:

1. While double-tonguing at medium (eventually high) speed, inflate the cheeks sightly. Firm the lip muscles right at the sides of the aperture before the inflation is begun in order to minimize changes in the sound quality as the cheeks inflate.

2. Bring the back of the tongue up to the rear of the hard palate, and, with a "pooh" articulation, use the cheeks and tongue to expell about one-half the stored air. Immediately close the lips and repeat this process, using the remaining air to play the second "pooh" articulated note. Inhale while playing both "air in mouth" notes.

3. "Restart" with normally double-tongued pitches.

For triple-tonguing, use the same process of circular breathing during two *staccato* notes. It is impractical to store enough air to play three notes. Therefore, when triple-tonguing, use either "pooh-pooh-tu", "pooh-pooh-ku" or "tu-pooh-pooh".

Circular breathing while playing multiphonics is another area in which careful preparation of the embouchure before starting the cycle is extremely important. Beginning with some of the most resistant multiphonics, such as the twelfths produced with the regular third octave G, F and E♭ fingerings, the following sequence is suggested.[1]

1. Practice each multiphonic with the normal embouchure.

2. Practice each multiphonic with the cheeks inflated. As with single pitches, the work area of the embouchure will be at the center of the mouth when this is done.

3. Practice inflating and deflating the cheeks while holding each multiphonic.

4. Unlike when circular breathing on single notes, avoid circular breathing when changing from one multiphonic to another. Embed the circular breath inhalations into the sustained length of multiphonics. If this is problematic due to rhythmic or phrasing considerations, make sure to change from one multiphonic to another WHEN THE EMBOUCHURE IS NOT MOVING. This can be when the cheeks are fully inflated or when they are completely deflated.

---

1. For detailed instruction on the performance and practice of multiphonics, whispertones and other extended techniques, please refer to my book *Tone Development Through Extended Techniques*, Multiple Breath Music Co., New York, 1986.

Given below are examples from my composition *Flames Must Not Encircle Sides*, which is based on multiphonic trills and exploring the harmonics that emerge as the flute is played through various *tessituri* while trilling with the same fingering. Gradually, the main harmonic groupings are mixed with increasing speed. The following two multiphonic trills are among those that are central to the piece. Practice while trilling, and hold each for at least thirty to forty-five seconds as you use your embouchure to push the flute through the harmonics:

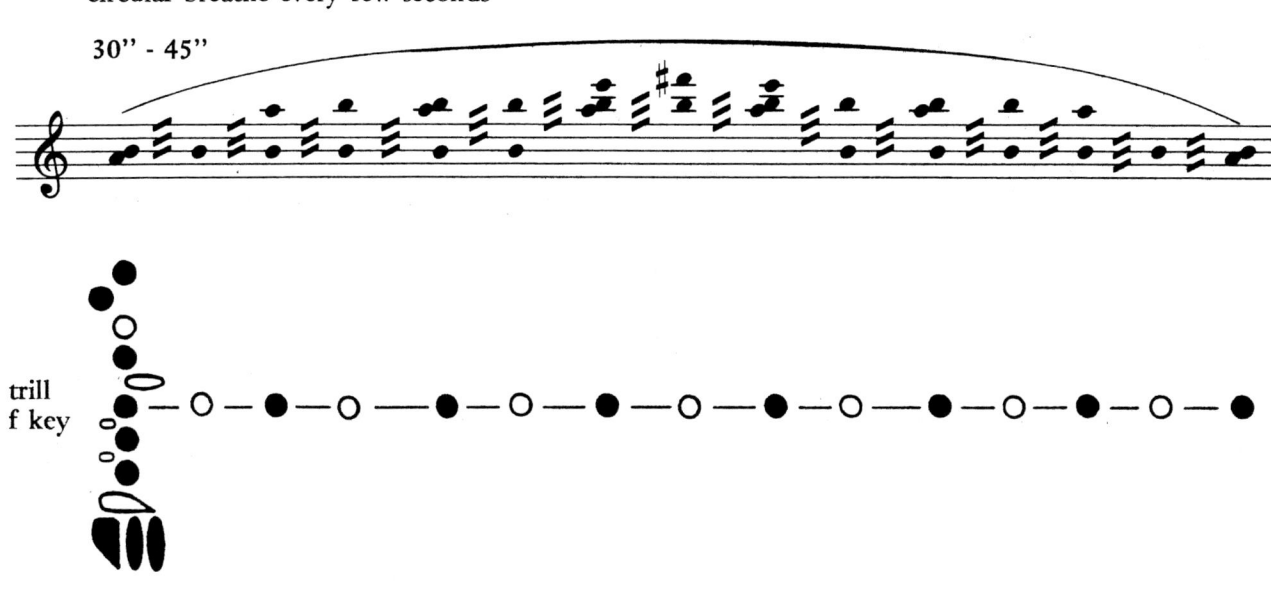

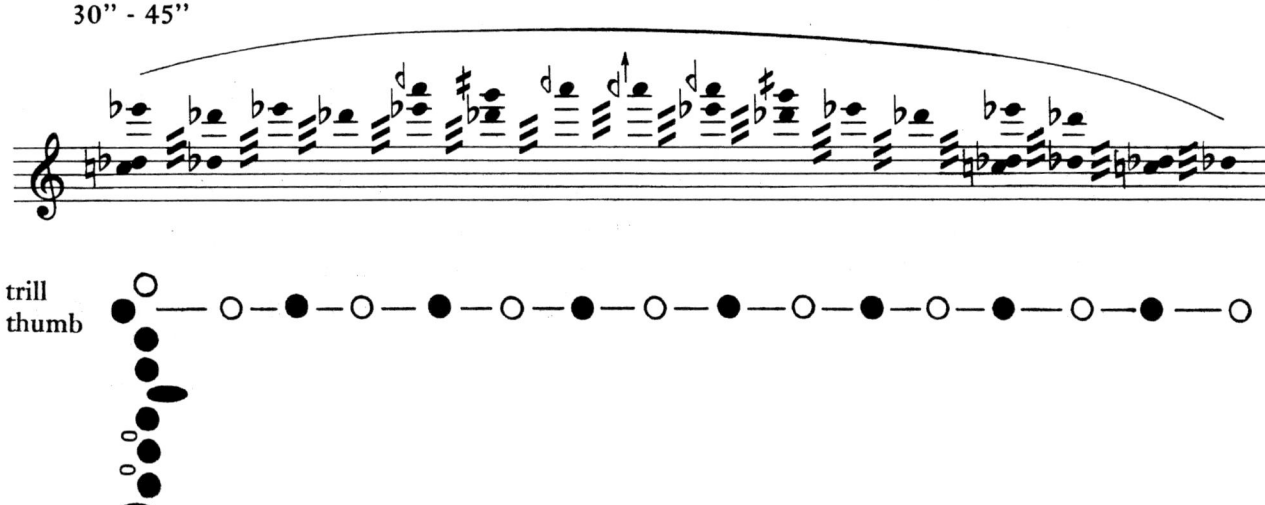

© *Multiple Breath Music Co., 1980*

Last in this chapter is a brief discussion of circular breathing while playing whispertones. This is the most difficult of all applications for circular breathing as whispertones use the slowest airstream, and thus the lowest air pressure, of all flute sonorities produced by blowing. Almost no cheek inflation is used when circular breathing on whispertones. Begin with practicing "sweeping" up and down through the overtone series of the low B and C. Inflate as much as possible, which in this case is a tiny bit, towards the top of the gestures. Then, carefully bring the tongue up and forwards, trying to match the speed of the air, before closing off the back of the mouth. Keep moving the tongue forwards while the back of it is in contact with the hard palate. Begin the release of the tongue while it still is moving forward, and "restart" the air with delicacy. Circular breathing on whispertones produces a ghostly, moving effect. Practicing this will lead to the most precise refinements of the mechanics involved.

finger low B throughout

# AFTERWORD

Whatever level we may be at as musicians—student or professional—we all should take the time to dream of where we would like to go in our playing, changes in sound, development of technique, pieces to learn and/or ambitions to realize. Thinking about the next days and weeks or the next decade, the important thing is to release the imagination, visualize goals, and harness the discipline, self-belief and drive needed to pursue our dreams. If I have been effective in getting one point across, I shall feel the efforts of creating the learning method and writing this book will have been well worth the time and energy spent, and that point is: the farthest flights of imagination *can be accomplished!*